Given A New
Life Twice

Given A New Life Twice

A true story of a Liver transplant Survivor

Dave Ryskamp

Library of Congress Control Number:		2013916809
ISBN:	Hardcover	978-1-4931-0090-3
	Softcover	978-1-4931-0089-7
	Ebook	978-1-4931-0091-0

This book was printed in the United States of America.

Rev. date: 10/07/2013

To order additional copies of this book, contact:
Xlibris LLC
1-888-795-4274
www.Xlibris.com
Orders@Xlibris.com
131157

To the love of my life, Jennifer
I could not have made it through without
your love and care for me.

Thanks also to family and friends
for their support and many, many prayers.

A special thanks to Andrea Perron
and Lin Johnson for their
corrections of my countless spelling
and grammatical errors.

TABLE OF CONTENTS

PREFACE

I T WAS NEVER my intent to author a book. I am a builder by trade, and apart from times reading blueprints and writing quotes, you won't find me behind a desk. But throughout the past year, God has been making it clear to me that I am to let Him make the choice of the tool in my hand. For now, he has called me to lay down my hammer and pick up a pen. God has given me a story to tell, with one purpose—to bring Him praise and to share Him with those around me.

I was born and raised in West Michigan in a small town where family is important and just about everyone goes to church. Having been brought up in the church, a Christian school, and a great Christian home, I grew up hearing about God everywhere I went. At an early age, I put my personal trust in God and knew he was alive and active. Little did I know what He had in store for me.

My prayer is that this true story will bring you hope. Are you facing the impossible? Are you in a time of waiting, with no end in sight? Does the mountain in front of you seem too tall? This life is filled with trials and as Gary Thomas says in his book, *Authentic Faith*, "What if life is not meant to be perfect, but we are meant to trust the One who is?" I hope my story will encourage and remind you that God is real, He does care, and He wants to be your support and help. I know what you're thinking, "How can a loving God . . . ?" You fill in the blank. Before you ask that question in regards to your own situation, join me on a journey. This journey begins and ends with a God who is faithful, with a promise to never leave us. God wants to use the hard things of this life to draw you closer to Him and make you better. He wants to turn your difficult situation around and use it to reach out and bless others.

1. A DIAGNOSIS

GROWING UP I was a normal healthy young boy who did everything just like everyone else. I was involved in every sport and activity available to me, from basketball to backpacking and everything in between. I went to a small Christian school where anyone and everyone made each team making life busy. I was very competitive and being the third boy in the family, I had to keep up. We were raised to be the hardest workers around, and in our family you did not slow down. I was nine years old when I got my first paper route, and that was just the start of multiple jobs throughout school and the rest of my life.

When I was 14 years old and in the eighth grade I started getting pain occasionally in my stomach area. The pain would come on for a little while then go away. As a teenager, I just gritted my teeth and pushed through. But as the months went on, the pain became more intense and would last for longer periods of time. The pain got to be so bad that I would be huddled over holding my stomach for a couple hours at a time. My mother is the type who would not rest until she figured out what was going on with her son. She got me in to have some tests done and the doctors discovered that I had ulcerative colitis. UC is a condition where ulcers in the large intestine bleed, causing pain, and other gastro-intestinal problems. Patients with ulcerative colitis have a 60% higher risk of cancer, so a yearly test is done to keep an eye on it.

I was given meds to help with the pain and bleeding; they worked great but did not help the diarrhea that came at least seven times a day. Still, it was wonderful to be without pain, and I learned to adjust to the sudden urges and knew where the bathrooms were at all times.

While testing for ulcerative colitis, doctors noticed that it looked like I had liver problems as well. The doctor at that time thought I had primary sclerosing cholangitis. "Primary sclerosing cholangitis, or PSC, is a rare liver disease that causes the bile ducts inside and outside the liver to become inflamed, scarred and blocked. As this process continues, liver cells die, and scarring (cirrhosis) develops. Eventually, the liver begins to fail, and a liver transplant is needed. People with PSC are also at a high risk for developing cancer of the bile ducts (cholaniocarcinoma)." (The Morgan Foundation. www.pscfoundation. org) No further testing was done at the time, and they were just going to keep an eye on it.

By the time I was 16, my blood levels had gotten worse and it was time for a test to confirm or deny me having PSC. My doctor did a liver biopsy which is taking out a piece of my liver and testing it for the disease. When the results came back we met with the doctor to hear the news. The results did confirm PSC, and in that small patient room he proceeded to tell me what he knew about the disease. He explained that there is no treatment for PSC, so he was going to put me on a medication for a similar disease in hopes that it would slow down the damage that was happening. The doctor said that PSC was a rare disease, not much was known about it, and the average age of diagnosis was mostly older patients. Only about 3 in 100,000 people get this disease. Because I was only 16, he did not have much to tell me. He said many patients with PSC were 40 or older, and he did not know what to say to someone so young. It was the year 2000, and he told me that in 2-40 years I would die if I did not get a transplant. I looked at that meeting as a blessing from God. It was not that I was guaranteed to die soon, but when you're told you have 2-40 years, you only hear two years. The diagnosis brought a real seriousness to my life. I had goals and dreams that I wanted to achieve, and I spent my time learning and doing things that moved me closer to those. I took my walk with God very seriously and wanted to live my life for Him in every way. It was during this time that I chose my life verse: 2 Chronicles 16:9a, "For the eyes of the LORD range throughout the earth to strengthen those whose hearts are fully committed to him."

Even at the young age of 16, I understood the fact that God had made me this way for a reason. Psalms 139:13-16 says, "For you created my inmost being; you knit me together in my mother's womb. I praise you because I am fearfully and wonderfully made; your works are wonderful, I know that full well. My frame was not hidden from you when I was made in the secret place. When I was woven together in the depths of the earth, your eyes saw my unformed body. All the days ordained for me were written in your book before one of them came to be." God does not make mistakes, and He had a great purpose for my life.

The last two years of high school went well, with only a few medical tests, including a visit to Mayo Clinic for examinations and testing. After high school, I went to Word of Life Bible Institute for a year in upstate New York. After graduating with my Bible certificate, I went back to Grand Rapids, Michigan, to attend the local community college for business.

While in high school I had visited another church youth group with a friend, and the moment I walked through the doors my eyes locked on this beautiful blonde named Jennifer. I could not get her off my mind. I was too nervous to talk with her, and since I thought I never had a chance with her, I didn't ask her out. But I kept going to that youth group and looked forward to seeing her every week. We ended up dating other people during high school. When I came back from college in New York, I decided to attend that church again and get plugged in. The first Sunday back I saw Jennifer again; she was even more beautiful—and single! We attended a college Bible study together and carpooled with others the 45-minute drive each way. After a while it was just the two of us riding out to the Bible study, and we never missed a study. We would talk about anything and everything together. After a few months, my brother asked me if I liked Jennifer, and I said no. (I was living by the big river in Egypt—D-Nile.) After that question I started to think more and more about her. I realized we had everything in common and believed the same way on everything. Turns out I really was crazy for her; I would go out of my way just to talk to her and be around her. In his book *Boy Meets Girl*, Joshua Harris says, "Run at God as fast as you can, and if you see someone of the opposite sex running in the same direction, then take a second look." I was running full bore after God, was very involved in ministry, and was not even thinking much about dating. But it was God who brought this beautiful woman running next to me, and I was no dummy. It was not long before I asked her out, and from our first date I knew she was going to be my wife. We had a whirlwind romance as I wooed her as best I could. Surprisingly it worked!

After 9 months of dating I knew it was time to propose. I had to plan something big so she would say, "Yes." I hung a huge banner on the top of a grain bin that read, "Jennifer will you . . . ?" Then I rented a plane and we flew by the mill and I popped the question in the plane. She was shocked and had to say "Yes" because it would have been a long fall out of the plane. I was excited when we got engaged because we could now hold hands. We had set standards that we wouldn't hold hands until engagement, and we would save our first kiss for our wedding. I got a lot of grief for these standards, and friends joked that

I would pass out on my wedding night after kissing. These standards opened a lot of doors for sharing Jesus with others. I remember telling someone our standards when I was then attending a local community college, and he was in shock. He yelled to some of his friends to come over and hear this, and next thing you know I was surrounded by about a dozen college kids. They were shocked, having never heard of such a thing, so I also took the time to tell them about Christ and the difference He could make in their lives too. The guys I worked with would say, "How can you know if you are compatible if you don't sleep with her before marriage?" I would laugh and say, "We'll have our whole lives to figure it out."

As an engaged couple, Jennifer and I spent a lot of time developing our relationship. We read books on marriage and finances together. We went to marriage conferences, went through workbooks, and talked through everything. By the time we got married, nine months later, we knew everything about each other. Many people talk about how hard those first few years of marriage are to adjust to each other, but we can't relate. I believe those first few years were very easy on us because of how deep our relationship was by the time we got married.

My health was something we talked about, but so far things were going well and there was not much to discuss. My doctor said that one day it would just hit me and I would need a transplant. Until that happened, I could live a fairly normal life. God had something he wanted to teach me, and one of those things concerned who was going to be in charge of my life God—or—me. God wanted to get me to a place in my life that I could agree with this verse in Jeremiah 10:23, "I know, O Lord, that a man's life is not his own; it is not for man to direct his steps." I had goals and plans for my life and thought I had it all figured out. Sometimes as Christians we live with limited surrender in our lives, but being a follower of God means total surrender. He gets to call all of the shots, not just the ones we let him.

I was currently working as a building products salesman and six months before we got married I started building a house for us and a house for my brother as well. This was an extremely busy time for both of us. Jen was very busy planning a wedding, finishing up nursing school, and helping me work on our new home. She finished up school, and I finished building both houses a week before we got married. We were excited and ready for marriage and a break.

DAVE RYSKAMP

2. THE HONEYMOON

WE GOT MARRIED on February 25, 2006, and the wedding went great thanks to my wife's thoughtful planning. After we were married, we packed up and headed to the airport to fly to Hawaii! It had always been Jennifer's dream to go to Hawaii for her honeymoon, and it was finally coming true. We were booked for one week in Maui and one week in Kauai. Our plan was to get as much sight-seeing done in the first few days, and then spend the rest of our time relaxing on the beach. In the first couple of days we traveled the road to Hana, explored the island, visited a black sand beach, and tried some local restaurants. Our third night on Maui we went to a traditional Hawaiian luau, and the food was amazing! The luau ended late that night, and we walked the beach back to our hotel. While we walked we talked about how excited we were to go whale watching and snorkeling the next day. During our walk though, I started getting a slight pain in my chest and liver area. Once back at the room I had to lie down on the bed because of the growing pain. I thought at first that maybe I had eaten too much food. (An all-too-common thing for a Dutch boy at an All You Can Eat Buffet!) But the pain was throughout my entire torso and was gaining in intensity. After a while, I thought my body was going to explode! The pain was getting so bad that I told my now-very-worried new bride that we had better go to the hospital. We made the drive to the other side of the Island and found the only hospital. Once inside we explained my detailed health history to the staff, and they ran the basic tests to make sure everything was OK. It was determined that it was my liver acting up and the debate started as to what should be done from here. Jennifer had recently graduated as an LPN and was well versed in how a hospital should run. The room they put me in was a shared room with another patient, which was not a big deal. What bothered us the most was not the dried blood on the wall next to my bed; it was watching a doctor change my roomate's dressings. My roommate must have had some kind of surgery or incision in his stomach area. The doctor walked in, and with bare hands pulled the bloody dressings off my roommate, redressed his wound, threw the old bandages away, and walked out of the room to visit the next patient without washing his hands. After we saw that, we insisted that they do no more tests. We asked them to get me comfortable and fly me home for tests. My doctors back home agreed and recommended I fly right to Mayo Clinic in Minnesota for further testing.

The Maui hospital policy was that no one was allowed to visit any patient past 9 p.m. So having only been married a few days, my wife had to leave the hospital and drive across to the other side of the island to our hotel where she was all alone. This was very hard on me as a man. Here I was, her protector, responsible for her, yet I was totally helpless. Our cell phones had no service, and it was a 45-60 minute drive to the other side of the island. I called out to God, "O Lord, please protect her!" It was then that God taught me how little I could control life's situations. God was in the process of teaching me some valuable lessons. And don't forget Jennifer. She was crying during the drive back, all alone and praying to God for protection. He heard both of our prayers, and every night that we were apart he protected her much better than I could have. If being booted out of the hospital and sleeping all alone was not enough, our hotel ended up kicking her out as well, due to it being too full. Jennifer then had to try finding another place to stay, besides packing up all by herself. The hospital decided to keep me for about three days for observation before they allowed me to fly home. Jennifer and I like to joke that we had a beautiful view of the mountains (when my roommate moved his curtain) during my stay in the hospital. But I never thought I would have to share a room with another guy instead of with my wife on our honeymoon. God has such a sense of humor!

Once out of the hospital, we had to look for a hotel to stay in because ours was booked solid and they would not let us stay. Our time on the Island of Maui was over and we missed our flights to Kauai. We had a flight booked to head home and needed to stay one more night. Most of the hotels on the island were booked leaving few choices. We were smart enough to have bought trip insurance, knowing that I was not the healthiest guy. We remembered reading that the insurance would cover hotel costs for trip interruptions related to health. So we did what anyone in our situation would do: we found the nicest and most expensive hotel on the island, and it had some rooms available! The cost of $475 per night did not bother us since we knew insurance would cover the cost. It turned out there was a clause in the policy that did not cover our expensive hotel room after all. But we sure enjoyed it before we knew that! We were able to switch our return tickets to fly out a week earlier

DAVE RYSKAMP

than planned, but the airline would only fly us back to our original destination and not to Mayo Clinic. So we arrived home to our waiting families much too soon. We then repacked our bags and started the nearly 10-hour drive to Rochester, Minnesota from West Michigan.

We had called ahead to our insurance company to let them know our plans so that our approvals would be in place. At the time, we had to get approval before undergoing any testing, or the insurance would not cover the tests. We arrived at Mayo and checked in. Upon arrival, they informed us that insurance had not approved us yet for any tests. They said the first test would cost $3,500 if we wanted to start before insurance approval. This was about twice as much as was in my savings account then. (I like to remind my wife of those great lines in our vows, "In sickness and in health, for richer or poorer.") I asked what my other options were, and they explained that I could sit down in this huge room with everyone else and wait for insurance approval. I looked around the room and saw about 75-100 people with dismal looks on their faces. Turning back to the lady behind the desk I asked her how long the other patients had been sitting there. She replied, "Some people have been waiting days, and others a couple weeks!" She then explained that she would call us back up when our insurance gave permission. We sat down stunned. "A couple of weeks?" I said to Jen. We started praying for permission from the insurance company. After only sitting there about 5-10 minutes our names were called out over the intercom. We rose to our feet and looked at each other with shock! Everyone else in the room looked at us with shock also. We got looks that said, "You just sat down, and now you're approved already? We have been here for weeks!" We went to the desk and were told that I was approved and could report for testing. We left the desk praising God for the miracle he had just done that day!

After a couple smaller tests, it was determined that I needed a stent put into my liver to open up one of the large ducts allowing for bile drainage and to relieve the pressure. The disease was in full effect and my ducts were narrowing and getting clogged. While receiving stent placement in my liver I ended up getting pancreatitis as well. This meant we had the luxury of spending another three days in the hospital as I recovered. We were very thankful that Mayo Clinic allowed Jennifer to sleep in the room with me. After recovery, I was released and we started the long drive back home to Michigan.

Our Wedding February 2006

Honeymoon in Hawaii 2006

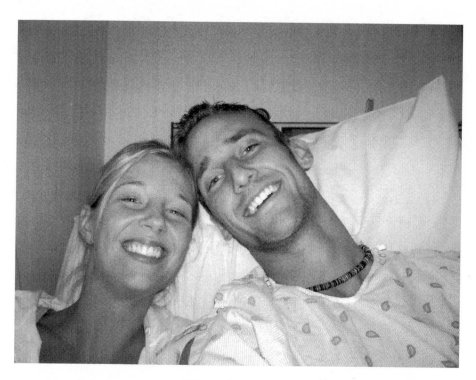

Hospital in Hawaii

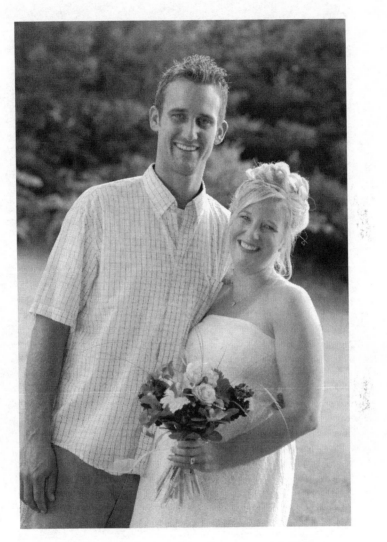

6 months before transplant. Pregnant with Kylor

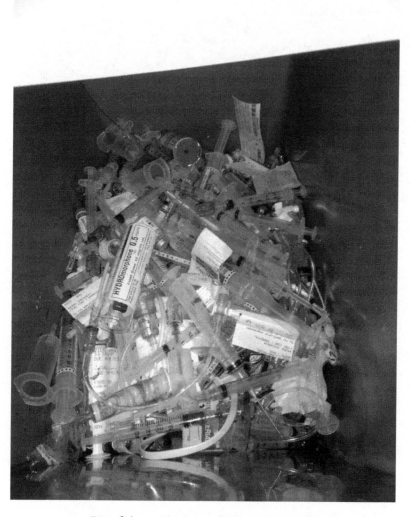

Pic of the meds given after 1 day in ICU

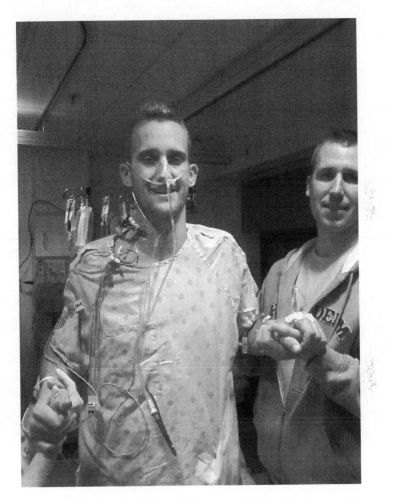

Dave in ICU with his brother Derrick

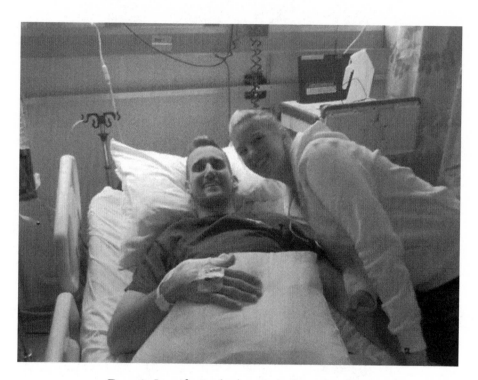

Dave & Jennifer in the hospital after transplant

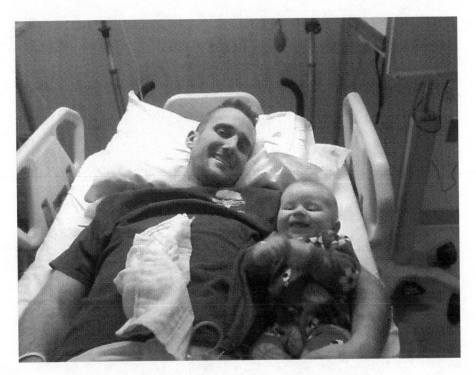

Kylor hanging out with dad . . . such a happy baby

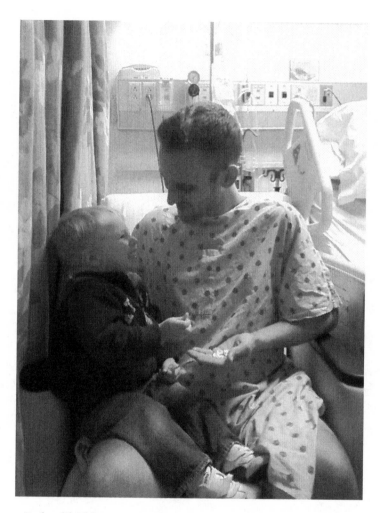

Zadan liked his visits with dad . . . and the candy helped too

Leaving the hospital on day 6

At home again!

Havyn Lynn born July 2013

Zadan(3), Kylor(22months), Havyn(2wks)

Family Picture at Jen's brother's wedding September 2013

3. WAITING

S O FAR WE had not been able to spend much time as a married couple and were looking forward to being just the two of us. Not long after we were home it was time to go back to work; my two week vacation was over. When I reported for work my boss wanted to have a meeting. He informed me that the company was not doing well and that I was laid off. I could not help but laugh. When in a situation like this you just learn to roll with it and find humor to be the best medicine. My boss felt bad; I knew it was not his fault and told him it was OK.

God has a plan and purpose for everything, and when you face a hard situation through no fault of your own, you need to look at what the Lord is trying to teach you and what he may have for you next. God's hand is in everything! If you are so focused on yourself you will miss the things he is doing all around you. Now I was out of work, my wife had just finished school, and we were three weeks into our marriage. Before we got married I told Jennifer that there is never a dull moment in my life, and I still have to remind her of that sometimes. Thankfully Jen quickly got a job in a doctor's office, and I got a full-time job working for a local builder. Both of our employers were very flexible with our schedules and were such a blessing to us. I had to spend a lot of time that first year in and out of hospitals, and they were always willing to let us have the time off we needed.

It was not long before the pain I experienced in Hawaii was back. After much research on liver programs, we decided to switch hospitals to the University of Michigan. U of M was one of the best for liver transplants, and it was only two and a half hours from home rather than nearly ten. The switch ended up being such a God thing, because we needed go to the hospital a lot! We then went to U of M when the pain returned in my chest and liver area; after some testing it turned out that the stent put in at Mayo Clinic was already clogged. This was the start of multiple stents that U of M would put in. The stents would get clogged, and then they'd be taken out, and the whole process would be repeated.

About halfway through our first year of marriage the economy started to go bad. This was the start of a terrible time in the construction trade. My new boss met with me and said that work had dried up and he was sitting on too many spec houses; therefore he no longer needed me. It was end of the summer of 2006 and I thought this would be a great time to start my own business building homes. I did not think much about how slow construction would be during the coming winter or how the next few years would be the worst time to start a construction business with Michigan's coming recession. Someone forgot to tell me those facts and I was determined to make my own business happen.

A few days after passing my builder's license test and getting an official company up and running, I was back in the hospital with pain. It was determined that this time my gallbladder was swollen, and after a couple of days of testing in the hospital I finally told the doctor, "Just take it out!" So he went in laproscopically making four small cuts, but it was too large to get out. He then had to do an open cholesectomy. (That means a lot more pain and a 9-inch incision across my stomach.) It turned out my gallbladder was three times larger than normal, and it was the biggest that U of M had ever taken out! ("Go big or go home.") Now a guy with a 9-inch cut across his stomach cannot do much construction work until it heals. It took a couple months of recovery before I could do any moving, not to mention lifting. I did my best to work anyway, causing myself an incisional hernia which I had to live with for the next five years.

On December 1st I was at home recovering from the surgery when Jen came home for lunch. I had just finished going over our budget and realized that we had no money left. Not much of a surprise since I was not working and Jen was off work while I was in the hospital. I told her, "Guess what honey? We have no money to spend on groceries the rest of the month." She smiled and said, "OK." She returned to work without knowing that the doctors and nurses in her office had taken up a collection that week for us. She was handed a $250 grocery store gift card when she returned from her lunch break! She called me bawling. God was waiting for us to realize we had no money, and had prepared in advance to answer that need within minutes! God is so big and loves to provide for our needs and show that He cares.

My wife and I joke that during our entire first year of marriage we lived in a hospital. But really, it was not much of a joke. For us, going to the hospital was like getting groceries—something you had to do on a regular basis.

After putting in and taking out over four more stents and treating more pancreatitis, meaning prolonged stays in the hospital, my doctor told me, "I cannot help you anymore. Your liver is so bad, you need a transplant!" The stents had bought us some time, but I now desperately needed a new liver. (Some people can go years longer due to the help of stents to open up ducts.) I was then recommended to the Liver Transplant Team.

In our second year of marriage I started a whole new battery of tests. It seemed like I had to do everything all over again. I underwent any and every test relating to the liver. I met with transplant survivors, social workers, and insurance staff. After everything had been done I was put on the transplant waiting list January 2007; so began our next journey.

Many people don't know much about the liver. For starters everyone has only one liver. I had many nice people come up to me and offer me one of their livers and my reply was, "OK, thanks, I will trade you for one of my hearts!" This always gave me a good laugh, and people were so nice to offer. "The liver is one of the largest and most complex organs in the body. It weighs approximately 1,500-1,800 grams (or about three to four pounds) and is made up of a spongy mass of wedge-shaped lobes. The liver has numerous functions that are necessary for life. The liver helps process carbohydrates, fats, and proteins, and stores vitamins. It processes nutrients absorbed from food in the intestines and turns them into materials that the body needs for life. For example, it makes the factors that the blood needs for clotting. It also secretes bile to help digest fats, and breaks down toxic substances in the blood such as drugs and alcohol." (*www.hhs.gov*)

Receiving a match for a liver requires a couple things. The giver and recipient must be of the same blood type, size, and hopefully a close match in age. When you wait for a liver, you are waiting in a very long line. There are about 16,088 people in the U.S. right now waiting for a liver and about 6,350 who get one each year. Only 4.8 percent of those waiting are between the age of 18-34. A majority of them are older. (Stats are from *www.unos.org* as of August 2012.)

I was informed that a call could come at any time, so I needed to be packed up and ready to go. Priority on the list is always changing due to the condition of each patient. Every three months I was required to do new blood work to determine my placement on the list for the next three months. If I was in the top 10, it was recommended that I stay within three hours of the hospital. If I traveled further, I would be removed from the list while gone and put back on when I returned. Due to my condition, it was recommended that we wait to have kids, get on disability and wait for a call. I thank the Lord I was able to work as best as I could right up to the time of transplant without going on disability. This was a huge blessing for me, and I was so thankful for work.

During this time, I still went back and forth to the hospital because of pain, side effects, or regular appointments. We call this time in our life the "waiting". It was like the Israelites waiting in the dessert to get to the Promised Land. After about one year on the waiting list we got a call on my wife's birthday. They had a liver for me! The liver is only good for a minimal amount of time before it goes bad, and since we had to drive two and a half hours we had to hurry. We called our family right away and called friends once we were in the car. Jen and I had an amazing time of prayer on the way to the hospital. We got there quickly and started the prep for surgery. I was prepped and met the doctors who explained the procedure to me. While the operating room was made ready, family came to say their good-byes and my wife and I said our good-byes. As I was being wheeled toward the surgery room the doctor's pager went off. He stopped, looked at it, and turned to me with disappointment written all over his face. The liver was no longer any good. We were all in total shock. He then explained that a team of doctors go and harvest the liver. When it is brought back, it is looked over, and then right before surgery it is looked over again. That particular liver had passed the first inspection, but failed when it came time for the transplant. We left the hospital so thankful that the doctors did not put a bad liver in me, then we went back to our normal life of waiting.

During our third year of marriage (second year of being on the transplant list) we got another call for a liver. The nurse on the phone started to explain the procedure to me again. Abruptly, she stopped her explanation and said, "It sounds like you have a cold." I very slowly said, "Yeah." Getting a transplant has guidelines, and if you are sick going into the transplant, your chance of recovery is not very good. I understood that and quickly added that I had been on a prescription for three days and was turning the corner. She responded that she would need to talk to the doctor and we hung up. Jennifer and I started packing while we waited for a return phone call. (Yes, you read it right, we did not have a suitcase ready to go. How do you live with your clothes packed up for years?) Moments later, she called to let us know that the doctor would not give me the liver due to my cold. I hung up and told Jen the news. We talked about how God allowed me to have this cold at this time. It was not His timing for a new liver yet. We knew that God had a plan, and that His way was going to be best. We had to trust Him.

Jennifer and I would often talk about the transplant and wonder when it was going to happen. We used to joke and say, "OK God, the next month would be a great time to do it."

"We hope I don't get a transplant before we do such and such." God must have just laughed and thought in His mind, "Thanks for telling the Creator of the universe when is the best time."

We felt like our life was on hold at all times, and we could not move forward. We had been married three years and had the baby itch. Trusting God, we decided to start our family. Shortly thereafter we were elated to find out that Jennifer was pregnant! We now had to figure out our work situation around the arrival of our child. I had been running my construction business as best I could the last two and a half years, but had not yet shown a profit. I was just covering gas, insurance, license fees, new tools, a new trailer, and a truck, but had not brought home the bacon. On top of that, because I was self-employed we had our health insurance through Jen's work, and the only benefit I got was time off whenever I needed it. And this was without pay of course. How in the world would we stay afloat financially if Jennifer quit her job to stay at home with our child? We prayed about it and felt that God wanted Jennifer to be home to raise our baby. This child was God's gift to us and our responsibility. We knew that God would provide for all of our needs. He had proven himself faithful to us for years; how could we not trust God now? Corrie Ten Boom says it best, "Never be afraid to trust an unknown future to a known God." There were a lot of reasons for Jennifer to stay working. With no insurance, I could not get a liver transplant, and I had not made a profit yet in construction. We prayed even more and asked our parents their opinions. One said, "You are crazy to even think that way; Jen has to stay working!" The other said, "God will provide a way." They both wanted the best for us, but after more prayer, we made the decision she should quit. We trusted in a God who could work miracles.

Zadan was born in October, 2009. Immediately after his arrival, my phone rang off the hook with new construction work. It was like God had been waiting for us to trust Him, and as soon as we did, He just poured on the work! We were able to buy insurance from Jen's previous employer to hold us over for the next 18 months until we found something new. After that, we had no idea what to do about insurance. We tried hard to get a different insurance, because the rate of $1,800 per month was as much as we had made monthly together the year before. Every good insurance company that did not cap their coverage would not take us due to my pre-existing condition. But, God did another miracle before the 18 months were up, and we were able to get the proper insurance we needed at a much more affordable price!

The waiting continued. It was fall 2011, and I had been on the list for nearly five years when we welcomed our second son, Kylor. At this point my health was very poor. I was very busy with work, but in a lot of pain. My body was shutting down, and I knew it. I was only number eight on the list and knew that I had been called the other times when I was number one. Number eight on the list meant that I was eight on the list at U of M among those who had my *same* criteria and blood type. My eyes and skin had turned so yellow. I had been yellow for years, but I had digressed so much in my health to the point that I was getting weird looks everywhere I went. (I often told my wife that until she rooted for the University of Michigan instead of Michigan State my eyes would stay blue and yellow!) Another side effect was that I was constantly itchy from the bile coming out of my pours as it could not get out of my liver well. For years I had to wake Jen up at night to scratch my back. I was itchy over my whole body, and would scratch until my skin bled. I remember getting many weird looks in public. I laugh at it now, thinking of how funny I must have looked to others. My feet were so swollen that every night Jennifer would have to try pushing the fluid out of my feet so I could fit into my work boots the next morning. My legs were so swollen I could no longer fit into many of my jeans. My urine looked like Coca-Cola and I was constantly exhausted. After walking a flight of stairs, I would get winded. I was getting weaker by the day. Back in college, I had bench pressed 250 pounds. (I know, to some of you out there 250 is warm-up weight, but for a guy with long arms it's decent.) I had also been doing 100 push-ups at a time. Now, a few short years later, I couldn't do a single push up. Even picking up my toddler was a struggle. The liver helps with production of protein, and since mine was not working, my body was pulling the protein from my muscles, making me grow weaker and weaker.

"This is what the Lord says; 'Let not the wise man boast of his wisdom or the strong man boast of his strength or the rich man boast of his riches, but let him who boasts boast about this: that he understands and knows Me, that I am the Lord, who exercises kindness, justice, and righteousness on earth, for in these I delight,' declares the Lord." Jeremiah 9:23-24. The things I used to boast about were taken from me and I had to rely on God instead of my own strength. The pain in my chest/liver area was so painful it affected everything I did. Either the pain was a constant pressure like someone sitting on my chest or a sharp pain like someone pushing a knife through my liver. I remember bending over while roofing a house less than three months before my transplant and thinking that I was literally going to pop because the pressure on my skin was so great. I also still had an incisional hernia, which I had gotten after my gallbladder was taken out, and it had been constantly hurting for the last five years. The doctors wanted to fix it during transplant because doing it by itself might cause my liver too much trauma. These side effects of a failing liver became like normal life and I just learned to deal with it; I didn't have a choice. After so many years of symptoms I couldn't remember what it was like to be normal anymore.

DAVE RYSKAMP

4. THE CALL

IT WAS DECEMBER 14, 2011, and like any other day I had just spent the morning visiting my jobsites to make sure everything was running smoothly. I arrived home at 10:15 to my excited two-year-old Zadan, my beautiful wife Jennifer, and the very new addition to our family, three-month-old Kylor. After hugs and kisses I went downstairs to my office to make some calls, do some billing, and quote some jobs. About 15 minutes later my phone rang, and I recognized right away the University of Michigan's phone number.

When I answered, I heard my doctor himself; he quickly told me he had a liver for me and then gave me the details. A young man about 27 years old from another state recently passed away. The doctors from the local hospital there have already removed his liver and were about to put it into one of their patients, when 'all of a sudden' the patient became too sick to have the transplant. They were left with a liver they could not use. So right away they called U of M, giving them the details and asking if they could use the liver. U of M went down their list and the first seven people on the list ahead of me were women who were all too small to receive this donor's liver due its size. I was the eighth on the list and was the same size as the donor, so the liver would fit perfectly. Also, I was also only a year older than the donor and had the same blood type. Keep in mind that I had been on and off the top 10 list many times during the last five years, and the other two calls I had gotten for a transplant came when I was number one on the list. This just shows how God's timing is perfect, and that we have nothing to worry about knowing God holds all things in His mighty hands.

The available liver was rated a CDC high-risk liver, meaning that because of the donors' lifestyle it could have HIV or Hepatitis A or B. At the time of his death, the donor did not have any disease, but there was a chance he could have just been exposed with nothing showing up yet in blood tests. My doctor asked if I still wanted the liver due to the small chance that a disease could be passed to me. I asked him, "If I was your son would you tell me to take the liver?" "Yes, I would," he said. That was enough for me to hear, and I said I would take it. He then said a nurse would call back with all the details, but I should load up and get on the road to Ann Arbor. I then rushed upstairs yelling to Jennifer the good news. I found her in Kylor's bedroom doing something parents do a lot with a newborn—changing diapers. I quickly told her the story while she looked at me in amazement, all the while holding a baby wipe in one hand and two little ankles in the other. We quickly called our parents and started throwing clothes into our suitcases. U of M already had the liver on ice, and they would be waiting for me in the operating room. We had to hurry because a liver is only good for a short time on ice before it goes bad. We had experienced that three years ago, so you can believe me that we hurried

Once on the road, we wasted no time, surprising the staff by showing up so soon. The drive to U of M was always a good time for Jen and I to reconnect and pray together; this time was no exception. It seemed like the transplant might happen, but then again, there was this thought in the back of my head that said, "Don't get your hopes up yet." Everything was happening so fast that it did not seem real. I had been on the list now for five years and this was the third call. I figured that I would believe it when it happened. I didn't have a bad attitude, but at this point, it seemed like this was the way life was and would be for a long time. Jennifer and I understood that for me to wait five years for a liver was OK, because it meant the donor could enjoy more time with his family. In order for me to receive a liver, we were very aware that someone would have to die. We knew God's timing was perfect.

When you get a call about a donor's organ, you can't help but think of the family on the other end who just lost a loved one. My life was being saved at the expense of another's. My family's prayers were being answered while another family was stricken with grief. There were so many emotions swirling around. We were hopeful, yet cautious. We were grateful and thrilled at a chance for healing, but humbled by the horrific loss that this meant for another family.

We were once again completely in God's gracious hands, which is the best place in the world to be. It is in those times when you have absolutely no control that you realize how big God is, and you can begin to understand how He sustains you every day. Once at U of M, things moved quickly. Because the liver had been on ice for so long, there was not even time for me to shower. The nurse said they would clean me on the operating table. By the time I was prepped, our families arrived to say good-bye before I was wheeled into the operating room. I always thought saying good-bye to Jennifer would be different than it was. I thought she would be crying, and I would be trying to console her. Instead, I got choked up as we parted and she reassured me it was going to be alright. Later on I questioned her about it, only to have her say, "I was just trying to be strong for you, and I cried after you left." I think we were in such shock that we did not know what to think or expect.

Jen explains this moment from her perspective best in her own words:

As I walked away from that room, I did not know if I would ever see my husband again. Everything happened so fast and it was hard to take it all in. It felt like I was going through the motions but could not fathom reality. I began to sob, and I begged God not to take him from me. I did not want our boys to grow up without their dad, and I could not live without the love of my life.

I felt God saying, "Do you trust me? I know what's best."

"Umm, God, I trust you if you give me the answers I want, but what if it's bad news?"

He answered, "Do you trust me? I will never leave you nor forsake you."

"Yes, God, I trust you, and I do know that no matter what the outcome you are always there."

At once, this peace that passes all understanding came upon me and the fear left me. Surrendering to Him is so hard because the desire to be in control is so ingrained in my nature. However, I've found that surrender is so much greater than any illusion of control could ever be.

While being pushed to the operating room, I lay there, and it was like all the things in my life were played back in a movie for me to watch. During these times you realize that what matters in life is God, family, and others, and you are willing to get rid of everything else. You have probably heard the saying, "There is no atheist in the foxhole!" When people are in a near-death experience they seem to call out to "God." It is no different in the hospital. My roommates and doctors in the hospital all would acknowledge there is a God. At the end of your life, whenever that may be, you will think (if you have not already), what's next? If there is no God, and we die, then we're dead. But if there is a God, we should know what He expects of us before that meeting. While looking back over my life I knew right away that God is the only one to call out to for help. I was not scared, but confident that what God says in His Word is true. Psalm 139:16b says, "All the days ordained for me were written in your book before one of them came to be." I knew God was in control and I would not die one day sooner than he wanted me too.

Once in the operating room, I noticed right away how serious this was. There were more people in the room than I could count, all of them waiting to do their part during the surgery. They were moving perfectly around their spots, getting their equipment ready without saying a word. Once they were ready, they stood around me and waited for their queue. The Lord gave me such peace and I was very calm while lying on the surgical table and watching all of the monitors, taking in the hi-tech equipment, and seeing the doctors and nurses moving all around me. I checked the big flat-screen TV and read all my information on it. The three anesthesiologists wasted no time knocking me out after verifying that I was in fact Dave Ryskamp, and that I was here today for a liver transplant. (Now you might be expecting to read how I died and went to heaven and came back to tell you about it. Sorry, you are reading the wrong book. Keep reading though!)

Here are Jennifer's words on what occurred during surgery & shortly after.

Waiting . . . this I was used to. If you've ever been in a hospital you learn how to wait. The time seemed to go fairly quickly with all the family and my two boys to look after. About four hours into the surgery I broke down crying and asked the family to come and pray around me. We were crying and praying when the doctor interrupted our prayer. He said, "I don't mean to interrupt, but I think my news will make you all feel better." We looked up with tears running down our faces and then the surgeon said, "We are all done with surgery and Dave is doing great! The surgery went perfect, and once we hooked up the new liver it turned pink immediately and started producing bile right in the operating room! He only lost 1 liter of blood and normally a patient loses five. The old liver was the size of a medium beach ball, 1 ½-2 times the size of a normal liver. Normally 96% of patients have a breathing tube left in after surgery, but we removed Dave's in the operating room. The surgery could not have gone any better, the new liver is working well, and we are very excited." We were shocked and praising God; it had only been four hours, and they said it could take up to 12. God is so good!

5. RECOVERY

IN A BLINK I came to and realized I was in ICU. I was a little shocked at first because I thought the room would look different and I would be in some kind of bubble. I quickly noticed all of the extra tubes I had coming out of my body. It was so good to see my wife, my boys, and the rest of my family! The transplant seemed to have happened so quickly. All I could do was smile at my wife, ask for more pain meds, throat lozenges, and a water sponge! Everything happened so fast. If it were not for the incredible pain and a 14-inch cut in my side I would not have believed I just had a liver transplant. The amount of meds the nurses gave me was astronomical. It was needle after needle; it would be a full time job to keep track of everything that went into me. I did not care that some of the vials had a skull and cross bones on them. U of M knew what they were doing, and I just smiled as best as I could. My throat was so dry and sore from the tubes down it that I just begged for some water. When the nurse was not looking, Jennifer would sneak me a wet little sponge as often as she could.

I was in ICU just over a day before they moved me to a regular shared hospital room. This was another miracle, because normally a transplant patient is in ICU for 3-6 days before moving to a regular room. Not only were we shocked, but so were the doctors. They just kept saying that this was the quickest surgery and recovery they had ever seen. I felt like I was the show-and-tell for the med students to see. I had a liver team, gastroenterology team, and the floor doctor and his team all checking up on me. God had done another miracle in my life, and I knew I was alive to tell others about it!

Whenever I spend time in a hospital, I realize how others have it much worse than I do. I was fortunate enough to walk into the hospital with a smile on my face, and the way things were going I was hoping to walk out with one real soon. No matter what happens in our lives we can always find a reason to be thankful. In tough situations, I try to think of Job from the Bible. He lost all of his possessions, most of his servants, all of his children, was covered from head to toe in painful boils, had his friends turn on him, and his own wife told him to curse God and die. Job's response to all of these things was, "How can I expect good from the Lord and not the bad?" and he worshiped God! Job had a proper view of God, and he knew that life was not going to be perfect. We need to trust God through the ups and the downs. Hard times will come in life. We all have a choice to make when they come, and I chose to allow these things to make me a better man. I looked back to the many times God was always faithful, praised Him for what He was still doing around me, and looked forward to the things He had in store.

My recovery progressed quickly. By the second day, I was up and walking with the help of my brothers. Each day was another step forward, and I was excited to get home. It was not long at all before tubes, pic, port, and hoses started coming out one by one.

Our families were a huge help, and they were there every step of the way! They were a huge blessing to us and helped in any way they could. God worked it out perfectly! We had two boys, and each set of grandparents took charge of one of them while I was in the hospital. Jennifer was still nursing our 3-month-old every three hours, so my mom would bring him back for feedings. Jen's mom would watch our two-year-old and play with him out of the hospital, then bring him back for visits.

At this point we want to just praise God again because of the temperament he gave our boys. They are so well-mannered and obedient. They were both angels in the hospital and most people did not even know we had kids in the room. The hardest part for me was when Zadan would visit and not want to come near me because I was too scary with all of the tubes. It was a frightening thing for a two-year-old to see and understand. After the first couple of visits he warmed up to me, and I quickly realized I needed a plan to get him excited to visit. I was not much fun just sitting there, so I started the tradition of eating big Tootsie Roll suckers together everytime he visited. (Thanks to the help of Uncle Joe keeping me supplied.) I also started ordering Jell-O and sherbet ice cream so I could have that for him as well. It was nice to be on the "other end," feeding him lots of sugar before giving him back to Grandma and Grandpa. It was not long before Zadan was telling people, "Daddy got a new Liv-ver!" I would draw a scar on his stomach so he could lift up his shirt and show people that he got a new liver as well. You just can't beat that!

DAVE RYSKAMP

The next couple days went well and pain meds were decreasing. It was hard to keep track of all the meds I was taking. The nurses had a system of how long I had to take each one and were decreasing them each day. I was quickly taking laps around the hospital floor on my own. I was feeling great and ready to head home. I think the pain meds made me feel better than I really was. By day four I was requesting to leave, but I was told I had to stay a couple more days. Day six was my departure date, and I passed the written and physical tests needed to go home. The last thing I needed to do was to learn all the medication names and doses that I had to take each day. I could not even tell you how many meds I started on, but I was glad that I was down to 10 different meds by the time I left. There were also a lot of restrictions to learn before we were able to leave. Among them were: no hot tubs, rivers, lakes, ponds, oceans; no using a towel twice: no buffets; no grapefruit; be sanitary in food prep; constant hand washing; avoid fresh dug dirt, demolition, crowds, people who were sick, and people who came from or traveled to another country; and wear a mask for a while. After all of the discharge instructions, we were able to go home. It was the afternoon of day six and we were walking out. As we left, I said good-bye to another transplant patient who had a back-to-back transplant to mine. She was just walking out of ICU and was told she had another six days yet on the regular floor. We were shocked, and praised God that we could go home.

I attribute such a quick recovery to God just wanting to show off! It was no doubt that this was a miracle and everyone knew it. God was getting the glory He deserved, and I was doing my best to tell the nurses and doctors about my great God and how He could be theirs as well. Psalm 77:14 says, "You are the God who performs miracles; You display Your power among the peoples." The other thing I attribute it to was the power of prayer. God's people were lifting me up all around the U.S. It even made the radio. God answered in a huge way, and we are so thankful to everyone who took the time to pray on my behalf!

As I walked out of the hospital, God wasted no time keeping me humble. I was on a weight limit of 10 lbs. for the first six weeks, and 25 lbs. for the next six weeks, which meant I could hardly lift anything, including our stuff and our boys. So I stood there while I watched Jen do all the lifting and loading. On top of that I could not drive because of the narcotics I was taking. Have you ever seen that guy in a parking lot who watches his wife do the work and then gets in the passenger seat? Don't you just want to knock him out? Now for the first time I was "That

Guy." I made sure when I was riding that my face was hidden as best I could. God must just look down and laugh!

We arrived home five days before Christmas, and that was the best Christmas gift. It was so good to be home as a family again. I was so thankful for the little things taken for granted every day like sleeping with just my wife in the room, playing with my kids, sleeping in a bed without plastic on it, walking bare foot, taking a shower without sandals, putting on my own clothes instead of hospital gowns, moving around without tubes and a hospital pole, getting good food out of the fridge whenever I wanted, and living in peace and quiet without interruptions. My plumber even blessed me with a nice tall toilet so I did not have to bend over so far to sit down. (Don't laugh—you won't understand this unless you have been in my place and are 6' 5".) Within one week of being home I had lost 40 lbs. of fluid. My new liver was doing its job and bringing my body back to normal. After losing all this water weight, my wife looked at me and said, "This whole time I thought you had muscle, and it turns out it was just water." We got a good laugh out of that. The pressure on my chest and body was gone and my "cankels" disappeared! My eyes were no longer yellow, and my skin returned to a normal color. It was amazing; I can't tell you how many times my wife said, "Your eyes are so white!" Soon the black circles around my eyes were gone, and I was not itchy anymore! My liver levels looked great, and after a few months my blood levels gave no indication that I had ever had liver problems.

Looking back I still wonder how my wife held up through the whole ordeal. She had to take care of three boys: a three-month-old, a two-year-old, and a 28-year-old. Not only did she do an amazing job at that, she still kept up on meals, laundry, cleaning, and everything else. We prepared our own meals just because of my new diet, and my mother helped us by getting our groceries.

We still had to go back and forth to U of M on a regular basis. It started with a couple of times a week, and as time went by the visits became less and less frequent. Every time we went for checkups, the transplant doctor was just shocked and all smiles with my progress. I told him this is what happens when the Great Physician shows up.

I started walking through my jobsites the seventh day after transplant. It was great to be back at it again; and work is truly a blessing to have. I was, of course, wearing a mask which made talking to my customers difficult. We would have to step outside so I could talk to them with my mask off. I also was blessed to have a couple of people to drive me around

DAVE RYSKAMP

to my different jobs. It was kind of nice having a chauffeur, and we had a good time. It would still be a while before I would be able to do the physical labor myself. I know I worked too much when I was supposed to be resting, but work had to get done. I was anxious to get off my pain meds because they did not allow much sleep, and besides, I was ready to drive myself around. I recovered quickly and am so thankful to God for the healing. It happened so fast that it is hard to remember.

You can't go through all of this without knowing that God has a plan. He has been there every step of the way and has been so gracious to us. He says in Jeremiah 29:11-14a, "'For I know the plans I have for you', declares the Lord, 'plans to prosper you and not to harm you, plans to give you hope and a future. Then you will call upon me and come and pray to me, and I will listen to you. You will seek me and find me when you seek me with all your heart. I will be found by you,' declares the Lord."

God was bringing me to a better place—closer to him. Maybe this story will help you see what God is doing in your life. As I am writing this book it is December and very cold here in Michigan. My family and I had just loaded into the van to go get some ice cream for Jennifer's birthday. When we arrived back home I parked the car outside the garage and unloaded Kylor first. Then I went back and opened the van door to unload Zadan. I tried to get him out of his car seat but he kept wiggling and pushing my hands away. I said to him, "Let me unbuckle you!" He looked up at me with a serious face and said, "No, it is cold out there!" You see, he was comfortable in the warm van and did not want to go outside in the cold. I told him, "You need to let me take you out so I can bring you into our warm house; it is just going to slowly get colder out here in the van." He still refused, so I forced my way to unbuckle his seat belt and carried him through the cold and into the house. That is exactly how we can be with God. He sees that if He moves us from where we are comfortable right now and carries us through some cold, harsh weather, there will be a nice warm house waiting for us that is way better than a mini-van. You have a choice to kick and scream like a three-year-old as God brings you through the cold weather, or you can understand what he says in Romans 5:3-4, "Not only so, but we also rejoice in our sufferings, because we know that suffering produces perseverance; perseverance, character; and character, hope."

6. WHAT MATTERS MOST

NOW THAT YOU have heard the story about what God has done in my life, I'd like to share what God wants to do in your life.

A perfect holy God created mankind who was sinless but had a free will. In Genesis we find Adam and Eve made the choice to disobey God, bringing sin into the world. Romans 5:12 says, "Therefore, just as sin entered the world through one man, and death through sin, and in this way death came to all men, because all sinned."

Because of that choice, we don't get a choice; we automatically are born into sin. Psalm 51:5 tells us that "Surely I was sinful at birth, sinful from the time my mother conceived me." I was diagnosed with PSC, and it was something I did not choose to have, nor did I have any say in the matter. In the same way you and I were diagnosed with a sinful nature. In Genesis we find Adam and Eve were created with a choice to follow God or disobey him in the Garden of Eden. Because they chose to disobey, all of humanity are now born as sinners. You and I were conceived with a big problem called Sin, and you and I have continued sinning to this day. I know what you are thinking right now. Who are you to judge me? Just wait; don't get defensive yet. I ask that you just read the Word of God with me and see what good news it has for your life. Stick with me, it sounds like I am beating you up at first, but it gets better as I go along.

Romans 3:23 says, "For all have sinned and fall short of the glory of God." Let's say that you and I are going to stand on the shore of Lake Michigan and throw a baseball over to Wisconsin. You may throw it further than me, but we both will come short of hitting Wisconsin. In the same way, God has a standard of perfection, and we have all come short of His standard. The smallest things like lies, cheating, gossip, lust, or you name it, is enough to fall short of His standards.

Having PSC was bad news for me. I needed a liver transplant, or I would die. In the same way sin is bad news for all of us. God says in

Romans 6:23, "For the wages of sin is death." Our sinful diagnosis ultimately leads to death, separation from God forever.

You and I now find ourselves in a great dilemma. I could do nothing to earn a new liver; it had to come to me. In the same way you can't save yourself from your sin. A perfect God has to do it. Listen to what scripture says in Romans 5:19, "For just as through the disobedience of the one man the many were made sinners, so also through the obedience of one man (Jesus) many will be made righteous."

Scripture tells us the good news of our situation in Romans 5:8, "But God demonstrates His own love towards us, in that while we were still sinners, Christ died for us." I could not have received a liver transplant without someone dying, and you and I could not be forgiven of our sins without Jesus Christ dying in our place. That is exactly what He did. Christ literally took our sin on the cross and died in our place and rose again after three days to show he had conquered sin and death. Jesus is the ultimate living donor.

With this information, we are given a choice. Ephesians 2:8-9 says, "For by grace you have been saved though faith, and that not of yourselves; it is the gift of God, not of works lest anyone should boast." No one can earn salvation; it is a free gift. No matter how much good you do, it won't get you any closer. In the same way, I could not have earned a new liver; it had to be given to me. The doctors couldn't be bribed. I couldn't work harder or pay my way to a new liver. It was a gift! When the doctor called me and asked me if I would like this new liver, all I had to do was say "Yes." In the same way, Jesus wants to give you a new life, but you have to say "Yes" to Christ to receive his free gift. Acts 16:31 says, "Believe on the Lord Jesus Christ and you will be saved." Romans 10:9-10 says, "If you declare with your mouth, Jesus is Lord, and believe in your heart that God raised him from the dead, you will be saved. For it is with your heart that you believe and are justified, and it is with your mouth that you profess your faith and are saved."

If you want to make this decision, you can do it right now. Choose His free gift. Tell God that you are sorry for the things you have done. Ask him to forgive you for all you've done wrong, and tell him you want him to be Lord of your life. Surrender to Him and follow His will for your life. 2 Corinthians 5:17 says, "Therefore, if anyone is in Christ, he is a new creation; the old has gone, the new has come!" My life has changed drastically twice. Once when I was young and I accepted Christ, and again, when I received my new liver. I have been given both spiritual and physical new life. Eventually, my new liver will fail. My body, like yours, will age and decay. But God offers us life beyond this physical world.

If you make the choice for spiritual new life, you will never be the same. God does give you a great promise in John 5:24, "He who hears my word and believes in him who sent me has everlasting life, and shall not come into judgment, but has passed from death into life." It does not mean your life will now be easier. Your physical, day-to-day circumstances may not change at all. In fact, the Bible says that you will have trials, and that they have come to refine you. (1 Peter 1:6-7, James 1:1-4) Along with that God gives you an amazing promise in his word in Deut. 31:6, "He will never leave you nor forsake you." You will have someone to rely on for strength to help you through whatever you may face.

Maybe you already know Christ as your Lord, but do you take your relationship with Him seriously? Life is so short and James 4:14b says, "What is your life? You are a mist that appears for a little while and then vanishes." Are you living each day like it could be your last? C. T. Studd said, "Only one life, 'twill soon be past, only what's done for Christ will last." When I was lying on that operating table, I saw clearly that God was most important. Nothing you can think of will bring you greater satisfaction than being sold out for Christ and putting Him first in your life.

DAVE RYSKAMP

7. WHY I WROTE THE BOOK

A COUPLE OF days after surgery, I could not sleep, so I decided to walk the halls to pass some time. As I walked I prayed, and it seemed like God was right there with me, carrying on a conversation. He told me that I needed to write out my story so others could see who God is and that He is still doing miracles today. I knew it was God speaking to my heart, and it brought tears down my face. I was a little embarrassed, so I headed back to my room hoping no one had seen me. I knew then and there I had to write this, and I told others right away about this experience so that I would have some accountability to get it done.

Well, by day seven I was back to work and very busy. I was too busy to hardly even rest, not to mention write a book. It continued like this the entire year, and I was just trying to keep my head on straight. I know work is a blessing, but many times we make work a top priority, and it quickly takes the place of more important things. Satan can really attack in this area and use work and success as a covert plan to pull us from God's will. I knew in the back of my mind that I had to write the book, I just was not making the priority to set aside the time. I was doing construction during the day, and selling homes at night (I am a realtor as well.). On top of that, I still had to manage my rental properties and make time for billing and quotes. God still thought it was a priority and slowly started to get my attention. As time went by he picked up His pursuit. It started with just reminders in my mind on a regular basis, and translated into verses of scripture and sermons I heard. TV commercials would come on about writing a book, and different things would remind me. I still did not set aside the time, and God got more serious. I ended up losing most of my construction help, which made life really crazy, but made me stop and think. I then received an ink pen from a lady in China who read my Carepages and turned her live over to Christ as a result. (Carepages are a website for people in the hospital, so that others can check and see how a patient is doing.) The Chinese woman wrote me a letter saying I should use this pen to write out my story so other lives can be changed like hers was! Wow, that was a spiritual 2x4 to the face from God!

At that time I thought I had better wrap up my jobs before beginning to write, but I could not find another guy to hire. All I had left was a part-time guy and everyone else I asked was too busy with their own work. I started working overtime myself to get some jobs done. It was during one of those jobs that God decided to really grab my attention. I was removing an old window when it shattered, and a piece of glass fell and hit my wrist, making it bleed like crazy. I thought it was just a scratch, so I wrapped it up well with napkins and tape and finished installing the windows. When I got home that night, I showed my wife the little cut and it was still pouring blood. I could not get it to stop bleeding so I went to the hospital to get stitches. That glass cut an artery, and it must have nicked a tendon because I could hardly move my right hand for a couple of weeks. It was to the point that if I squeezed something my hand hurt, and I could definitely not swing a hammer with force. God had debilitated my right hand temporarily crushing my ability to work. Needless to say, He had my full attention.

I committed to stop work for a few weeks, and started pushing off or canceling jobs. I figured I could still just sub out some jobs and keep an eye on them while I wrote my book. It was then that my now one-year-old threw my phone in the toilet and ruined it. At this point, my wife and I were laughing and figured I'd better write the book before something worse happened. So then I did what most of us do to God. I prayed and gave him some excuses. I said, "Lord, what about our finances while I am off work writing this book?" I also told him that I don't know how to write or spell. There is a reason that I am in construction. (I wish you could see right now how many words spell check has underlined and how many fragments need revising in the rough draft of this book.) God was gracious to me and answered my prayers. The very next day we opened up our mailbox only to find a check, and it was enough for me to quit work for a while. We had not told anyone about our prayer the night before; it was God just showing us how big He is and removing any excuses I had. That same weekend we watched a sermon on-line from Pastor Bob Coy and it was titled, "Need a Miracle?" I knew this was for me and I prayed that God would do a miracle and allow me to write a book. I felt inadequate like Moses in the Bible, but I knew if God wanted this, then he would give me the words to write and provide a good editor!

Maybe God is trying to get your attention for something in your own life. It could be that He has something great He wants to use you to do, or maybe He is telling you that you need to get right with Him today. Don't be stubborn like me. Listen to His call.

8. LIFE AFTER TRANSPLANT

MANY PEOPLE ASK me how life is after transplant. To answer that question best would be to say that I am grateful to have life after a transplant! I am so thankful to the family who donated the liver, thankful to the U of M team of doctors and nurses who did an incredible job on my transplant, and thankful to God for sustaining my life. It has been a over a year now since transplant, and for the most part I am in very good health. I will be on meds for the rest of my life, and I use caution in certain areas, such as work environment, food, and personal contact. I have to still be careful when I work, as I am still not physically 100%. I have been able to do most things like framing, roofing, tile, and trim, among other things. I just have to work slower than usual and be careful to not hurt myself. With a little lifting and bending I am sore, but I assume that will go away with time. I am so thankful for this second chance at life. Life has changed and that is OK. I still get regular blood tests and meet with the doctors at U of M. I still am dealing with ulcerative colitis, and was just diagnosed as hypoglycemic. Life is not going to be perfect, but God has helped me through everything. God's Word says in Psalm 9:9-10, "The Lord is a refuge for the oppressed, a stronghold in times of trouble. Those who know Your name will trust in You, for You, Lord, have never forsaken those who seek You." May you trust God in your good times and in your times of trouble, because he is there! Laura Story in her book, *What If Your Blessings Come Through Raindrops*, puts it this way, "Some things in life are uncertain: health may vanish; wealth may disappear; success may be fleeting, and the victories we hold most dear may, in time, be transformed into bitter defeats. But in a world of uncertainties, one thing is certain: God loves us. And that one fact can make all the difference."

If you have any questions or comments regarding the book feel free to contact Dave at *givenanewlifetwice@yahoo.com*. We'd love to hear from you!

REFERENCES

The Holy Bible, New international Version (NIV) Copyright 1973, 1978, 1984, by International Bible Society.

Boy Meets Girl, Joshua Harris. 2000 Multnomah publishers, Inc.

What if your blessings come through raindrops?, Laura Story. 2012 Freeman-Smith, a division of Worthy Media, Inc.

Authentic Faith, Gary L. Thomas. 2002 Zondervan

DON'T

SHOOT YOUR

FUTURE

SELF

A PATHWAY FOR THE VETERAN'S TRANSITION

ERIC POWER

Drew,
ONE YEAR LEFT
HOMIE - LIFE IS GOING
TO HIT YOU WITH ALL AMURIQNES
IT has to offer!
Ⓔ

DON'T

SHOOT YOUR

FUTURE

SELF

A PATHWAY FOR THE VETERAN'S TRANSITION

ERIC POWER

Don't Shoot Your FUTURE Self

Eric Power

Copyright © 2021 by Eric Power

Printed in the United States of America

First Printing, 2021

ISBN-13: 978-1-951805-22-7 print edition
ISBN-13: 978-1-951805-23-4 ebook edition

Waterside Productions

Waterside Productions
2055 Oxford Ave
Cardiff, CA 92007
www.waterside.com

DEDICATION

To my wife, Chikako, thank you so much for dedicating your life to me and supporting me in all my crazy adventures! I love you, baby ...

To my mentor and father, Ralph, I could not think of a better way to honor you than creating a story around our interactions. I remember all the lessons you taught me. I am sorry I was not there when you passed away. You are forever missed and forever loved. Rest in peace, Pops; we've got the watch.

To my children, Leilanni, Maya, Mia, and the one on the way, due 5-16-2021, I will never give up on you and will always be here for you. I want you all to know that times will get tough, and through tough times, we find light. Remember you're loved and someday it will be your turn to pass the torch.

To my mentors, Greg and Marvin, thank you for your support, help, wisdom, and counsel along the way. I owe a lot to you both. Loyalty is Power.

TABLE OF CONTENTS

FOREWORD

I n an ever-changing world, we are both challenged and defined by the struggles that ultimately shape us. As an active combat veteran, Eric Power understands the unique challenges and sacrifices faced by servicemembers, but he also has had the fortune of being surrounded by mentors who helped him appreciate his true value and his potential.

In *Don't Shoot Your Future Self,* Eric shares these challenges and struggles through the story of David Little, a civilian veteran who encounters joblessness and uncertainty about his future. Through the caring guidance and mentorship of a stranger, David discovers that he has unique talents and strengths and uses them as he gains the experiences, tools, and lessons to become a successful entrepreneur.

More than a parable that shares business and success principles, you'll find this is an unforgettable story about life, relationships, and the power we all have to create a lasting imprint on the people we meet and know. Like me, you will be strengthened by the knowledge that while we all face challenges, they can be the steppingstones to a bright and promising future.

Let this book be the start to your future success and happiness.

Dr. Greg Reid

Award-winning author, keynote speaker, and film producer

1

YOU ARE TERMINATED

A newly separated veteran, David Little had proudly served his country for ten years. With a military career that included multiple combat tours in Iraq, Afghanistan, and other foreign lands, David now found himself struggling to transfer his military success to a career as a civilian.

It wasn't that he wasn't capable—he was, indeed. The problem was that his training was military specific; unfortunately, there seemed to be a lack of careers that aligned with his skills and experience. At 30 years of age, his resume wasn't very long; it didn't include a list of impressive credentials or accomplishments required to attract a prestigious position or income. While he had served with honor and pride, he was frustrated that his service hadn't prepared him fully for post-military success.

Nervous to begin this next phase of his life, David was willing to accept any job he could get. He needed the experience … and the money. After watching a personal development video on YouTube, he decided to pursue a career as an entrepreneur, the one career path that would allow him to have sole influence over his time, success, and happiness.

But there was one problem. David didn't have the skills and experience necessary to succeed. Knowing he needed experience, he accepted a position as a sales professional for a company that sold collegiate sports apparel. He quickly learned that selling was hard work. To make matters even more challenging, he wasn't a smooth talker. In fact, David was a man of few words and often felt uncomfortable being outside his house, especially when talking to strangers. He was used to being in full control. In the past, he'd been looked up to and respected. People moved when he spoke in the military. Most often, though, he didn't speak, per se. Yelling and using a firm tone were his mode of communication in the service, and when he did, people listened. Focusing on the mission at hand, he had spent the last ten years performing at a very high opt-tempo without outside interference. This did not work in the civilian life that he was struggling severely to comprehend. In fact, he had been terminated from a few jobs after the military.

Nine months with the company came and went before David had his first real opportunity to make a big sale. After building a relationship with the CEO and athletic director at one of the local universities, the CEO had asked David to send them a quote not only for new team uniforms and warmups, but also the equipment for a new multi-million-dollar field they were constructing. It was a single 2.12 million-dollar order. His commission would have been $212,000 alone. He'd spent the entire night at the office writing it up and had dedicated six months of his life to building this relationship. He personally took the CEO out to many dinners, fancy parties, and introduced him to a few high-performing business executives that helped him close multi-million-dollar side deals not associated with the college.

The next Monday, he was actually excited to go to work. Today was the day he was going to land that big deal. He could feel it! He was so sure of it that he didn't let it bring him down when he noticed that a button had popped off his shirt and after changing into another, spilled coffee and dripped egg yolk onto it, as well. He was on such a positive note that nothing could touch him. For the first time, it was finally going to happen! He was going to taste sweet success. It was all he'd talked about to his girlfriend over the weekend. He had met her on his last tour in Japan, after eight years of being stationed there. After not seeing her for ten long months, he had been super excited to share his enthusiasm about this deal with her, and she had echoed his excitement.

Now on his third shirt, he decided to leave before anything else could go wrong. After spending 10 minutes looking for his car keys, he realized he was pressed for time and ran out to his car, only to find that he had a flat tire.

With a long sigh, David told himself it was okay—he'd just have to take the bus. He texted his supervisor, letting him know he was going to be late and started the mile trek to the bus stop. The bus stopped at half-hour intervals, and he knew he could catch the next one, but only if he hurried. *At least it's not still raining,* he thought. *Thankfully, that's going in my favor right now.*

A bit winded from his quick pace, David let out a sigh of relief that he had made it in time, just as a bus was approaching. With his briefcase in his left hand, he stepped closer to the curb, not realizing he had situated himself perfectly for the unexpected — the bus flew through a puddle on the side of the road, leaving his shoes, pants, and third shirt heavily sprayed with muddy water, before it continued on its route without stopping.

"You have got to be fucking kidding me right now!" David exclaimed with military enthusiasm and still holding his briefcase, automatically threw his hands up in the air, staying true to his training to always be on the ready to salute. Angrily, he glared at the back of the bus as it rolled out of sight. What had started out to look like a promising day had certainly turned into an utter shit fest. Resigning himself to the fact that he had to go back home and change clothes again, he executed a perfect about face in military format, called his boss, who proceeded to yell and belittle him, and returned home to change.

By the time David arrived at work, he was two hours late and more than a little disheveled. He quickly logged in to his computer to check his email, and there it was ... the email he'd been waiting for about the university's order. Realizing that the athletic director hadn't texted him as promised, it didn't take long to find out why.

The email stated:

"David,

Thank you for your price quote.

However, at this time, we have decided to purchase our team apparel from another company.

Your Friend,

John Banner"

There it was, short and sweet. In just two sentences, he'd lost his biggest sale ever, without even stating a reason why they had opted to go with the competition. David was banking on this, as he was behind on bills and only $127 in his account. Reading the email again, he shook his head in disbelief. John had given him his word, and he'd trusted him to the point that he already had plans for the commission check. He wanted to bring his love over from Japan and marry her. In two seconds, his future was taken away. Not only did David have to come to terms with his life quickly falling apart, but he also had a hip side reaction and sent a very angry email in reply to John, the CEO of the company.

"John,

I don't know what is going on at the moment. Over the course of the last three months, you gave me your word on a few occasions that we would move forward. As you personally requested at dinner Thursday night, I sent you the quote Friday. We beat the competition prices by 10%, and I was able to get you another 10% off on such a large order. What's the problem?

Seriously, what the fuck brother? Are we not friends? Why the hell are you choosing another company whose prices are 10% higher than what you would pay with us? Especially after you looked me in the face and gave me your word?

I have taken you out to many nice dinners when I could barely afford to buy groceries, and this is how you are doing me?

I came over and helped you with your taxes and reviewed some contracts for you for free. This is how you are doing me?

Really, man, are you kidding me? What the hell is the matter with you?

Why can't you have the integrity and honor to commit to what you say and follow through? You call me a friend and cry to me on the phone about your divorce and you do this shit? You're not my friend. Friends do not do this. You knew I was banking on this to bring Mayumi over here! You video chatted with her and promised you would move forward!

At least give me a reason as to why you're screwing me over.

Not your friend,

David Little"

To say the next hour was uncomfortable would be an understatement. Sitting across from his boss's desk, he went through the questions he asked, one by one. Was he sure he had followed up with the AD and coaches? Had he given them promos and freebies or offered them all available company and vendor discounts? He had taken them out to dinners and very elite networking parties. There had never been issues with John or his college before. Why did he not follow through this time? Then, his boss asked him the loaded question—why did he send that email, which he instantly regretted? Unfortunately, David couldn't answer any of those questions. He didn't understand why, not at all.

"I don't know what went wrong," David admitted as he was speaking to his boss. "He gave me his word that this was a sure thing."

"It's never a sure thing until the money is exchanged. Chalk it up as a big life lesson learned. You should have hustled and got him to commit before you had a chance to be underbid," his boss said.

"I did have them commit. He gave me his word. He even gave my girlfriend his word on video chat, when I took her call while I was out to dinner with him. I don't know what happened," David continued.

"One thing you cannot do, ever, is respond the way you did via email. You not only brought dishonor on yourself for having a severe emotional reaction, which by the way, was not warranted, but you have also brought a black eye to my company. I don't know if we can ever repair our relationship and reclaim this account. For this reason, I must terminate you from your position," his boss said.

As instructed, David quickly packed his things and left the company. He continued beating himself up, and he did a really good job of it. Berating himself for letting the deal fall through and sending that email, he convinced himself that he was a loser. He told himself that he didn't have any people skills and that he would never make it. He even tried to convince Mayumi that she was better off with someone else. Yes, she admitted she was disappointed that their plans had to wait, but she said she was more concerned about him right now and asked him not to be so hard on himself. Usually, she knew how to calm him down, but this time, her words had no effect on him whatsoever. He even considered rejoining the military. He could just give up and go back on deployment, where things were normal. And who was he kidding, there was no way he'd ever make it as a sales professional, let alone succeed as an entrepreneur.

What more could possibly go wrong? What do I do now? he asked as he thought about his day. *I might as well face it; I just don't have what it takes to live anymore.*

In the military, David knew what to do when he fell short of his own expectations, but in his present circumstances, he didn't know what to do or where to turn. He had every reason to be upset ... being hard on himself was one thing he found that he was always really good at.

2

THE MENTOR

For years, David had been an early riser, always up at the crack of dawn, ready for the full schedule that awaited. Despondent and idle, he didn't know what to do with his time as he sat around and waited for the day to pass. The massive amount of negativity in his head was building, beating what was left of his confidence to a pulp.

A restless day after being terminated flowed into a painful conversation with Mayumi that night. He now had to face telling the love of his life that he was not going to be able to bring her over here as they had planned. He felt horrible, so much so that he expressed to her that he did not want to live anymore, that he felt like there was no reason to go on.

After hours of drinking and close to blacking out, the last words he slurred to Mayumi on the phone that night were, "I will always love you, Mayumi, and I am so sorry I failed you. Thank you for always being so sweet to me and showing me what love is. I don't deserve you. I have no money, and all I know is war and how to fight. I hope you find a good man who can take care of you."

After hanging up the phone, David grabbed his .45 and loaded it with hollow point shells. Picking up his gallon of Captain Morgan Rum, he went into the bathroom. Pausing to look at himself in the mirror, he screamed at himself for being such a fuck up. He kept asking, "Why is it like this?" As if he weren't alone, he begged out loud for help. Finally, he called his half-brother, who had always been his rock. Their conversation was short and filled mostly with David's severe emotional outburst. It was his brother who abruptly ended it with, "You should kill yourself; you're a waste on society." This was the last time David would speak to his brother.

David believed him, and looking in the mirror, he quickly swallowed some pain pills and anxiety pills he had been prescribed by the VA. Everything was starting to get dark, and he grabbed his .45 handgun and held it to his head with his right hand. With his left hand, he took another swig of the rum and screamed as loud as he could, as if he were channeling his guardian angels, "DON'T SHOOT YOURSELF!"

Just at that moment, David let go and everything went black as he passed out on the bathroom floor...

****

The next morning, David woke up to incessant pounding on the door.

"David… Hello, David…" a man yelled.

Startled, the noise was enough to lull David out of a deep sleep. Finding he was surprised, yet thankful, to wake up, he walked to the door to see who was there.

"I'm Officer Aaron Whlechel. Are you David Little?" asked a police officer in full uniform.

"Are you okay, son?" asked the second officer, who was standing beside his partner. David had no idea what they wanted, but he did notice that they seemed deeply concerned about something.

"Um, yes, I'm David Little. Hey, is it okay if I put some clothes on real quick? I'll be back in a minute," he said.

David went into his bedroom and quickly put on a shirt and a pair of shorts, wondering why there were two police officers at his door. *I didn't do anything wrong*, he thought—*except lose an account and my job.*

"Hi, officers, sorry about that. I was sleeping," David said.

"It's okay. We received a call asking us to do a welfare check to see if you are alright. We're glad to see that you're okay, but if we might ask, what's going on?" explained Officer Whelchel.

David sighed, then went into detail about his last few days and all the problems that had arisen. Then he began talking about his deployments and what haunted him at night about the war. At the end, he summed up his frustration, saying he just didn't feel like he fits in anywhere.

"This is all a normal phase of separating from the military," said the other police officer, who had introduced himself as Officer

James Daniel.

"I understand what you're going through. This is a very rough time in your life, but a permanent fix to a temporary problem is not a good solution, son. As veterans, we have it inherently more difficult, due to our programming by the military. You have to wake up every day and thank the universe for being alive," advised Officer Whelchel.

"Are you going to be okay if we leave?" asked Officer Daniel.

"Yes, sir, I will be," David replied, suddenly feeling a sense of hope because someone cared enough about him to have the police come over and check on him.

David said goodbye to them, but not before Officer Whelchel offered him his personal card and a number to call if he ever got that low again. After the police officers left, David broke into tears, crying because he was happy to be alive. He cried because someone actually cared about him. He cried because he knew that he had never been at such a low point before in his life, and he cried because there was nowhere to go but up. After about 30 minutes of releasing his emotions and letting things settle in, David took a shower and got ready to face a new day.

After filling his coffee cup, he killed some time scrolling through social media. Usually, he did a quick perusal of the posts, seeing if anything important caught his eye, but today, he wanted to read everything, even the ads, hoping to waste some of the time he had too much of, with a newfound look on being alive and what it actually meant.

He'd seen the advertisement countless times and had always

ignored it, never placing much credence in the simply worded offering, which said, "Free Business Consulting," followed by a local telephone number. *Yeah, right,* David thought. *Nothing is free, and if it is free, it can't be worth anything. It's probably just another gimmick to get some sucker to buy something. It has to be a scam,* he thought.

Dismissing the offer, David continued to scroll through his feed and then checked his email, with the slim hope that someone somewhere might have sent him good news. Who knows— maybe he had inherited a ton of money from some long-lost uncle in another country or perhaps someone out of the blue sent him an offer he simply couldn't refuse! *Fat chance,* he thought. Ever the skeptic, David knew if it sounded too good to be true, it probably wasn't.

The thought reminded him of the ad he'd read on social media. Free business consulting—three words with no explanation or details. David had seen the ad before and wondered if anyone had ever acted on it. Once again, he opened his feed and looked for it, noting that the post hadn't received a single comment, follower, or even a "like."

Just as I thought, it's probably not legit, he reasoned. Yet, for some reason, he was curious. What if it was legitimate? What if he could benefit from it? What did he have to lose? At the minimum, he figured it couldn't hurt to call. At the very least, it might help him kill some time; besides, he had nothing left to lose.

To his surprise, his call was immediately answered by a real person. Pleasant and professional, a woman said, "Good Morning, Ralph Power's direct line. May I ask who is calling?"

After giving his name, the woman asked him if he was available for an appointment the next morning. Although David attempted to get the woman to provide him with more information about the offering, she refused, simply stating that there was an opening at 10:00 a.m. the next day if he could make it.

Taking the appointment, David grabbed a pen and quickly jotted down the address, noting that it was in a prestigious part of the city. The lady had told him to take the elevator to the penthouse on the top floor. This puzzled him even more; he would have been less surprised if he'd been directed to a seminar in a second-rate hotel conference room.

That night, he told Mayumi what he had done the night before, and she pleaded with him to never do anything like that again. She told him she didn't care about money, that his heart was what she loved. She gently reminded him that he had so much to offer the world. Nothing mattered, as long as he was okay. It broke her heart to hear that David had tried to kill himself and that he'd almost joined the 22 veterans a day that do succeed.

Then, he turned the conversation to the ad and the appointment he had made. Hoping this would be just what he needed to turn himself around, Mayumi encouraged him to follow his heart and his intuition. But she felt like she could hear some hesitance in his voice.

"You sound very hesitant, honey. Are you considering cancelling the appointment?" she asked.

"I was thinking about it. It is difficult to leave the house. Then again, a part of me wants to go. I feel like I have to go—like I have to meet this man. After all, what do I have to lose?"

That thought stayed with him until the next morning. After he showered and shaved, he wondered how he should dress for the meeting. Since the only information he had was the address, he pulled out a sport coat and tie, hoping to hit a happy medium between being either too formal or casual.

Oh, well, it'll have to do, he thought as he walked out the door.

Remembering the fiasco he'd encountered a few days before, David decided to drive to the appointment. While the bus would have been less expensive than the exorbitant downtown parking fees, he didn't want a repeat of any part of that day. Today, he hoped to avoid the unexpected.

But that was precisely what he walked right into. As soon as he stepped off the elevator into the penthouse hallway, his shoes sunk into the plush carpet, making no sound as he made his way past a professional sign that said, "Welcome, David Little. We are pleased to have you, sir."

Where am I, David wondered. *I feel like I've stepped into a fantasy land. This cannot be the correct place. Not for me.*

Double doors adorned on each side by a brass lion whose poses were frozen in a mighty roar caught his eye, and as he approached them, he tried not to let out the silent whistle of admiration that threatened to escape. The lions were regal and elegant. Their perfectly coifed manes were sculpted into magnificent works of art that personified dignity and beauty, rather than beasts of the jungle.

Taking a deep breath, David raised his arm to reach for the door knocker, only to have the doors open, as if on command.

"Welcome, Mr. Little. We have been expecting you," the immaculately dressed woman said with a smile. "Please do come in."

Stepping inside, David took in the surroundings. His initial impression was one of money, but then he realized he was wrong—no, this place represented wealth and timeless class. It was a stately room, both elegant and classic, the kind one would expect to see ... well, he didn't know where. He had never seen anything like it before.

"Come this way, please. Mr. Power is waiting for you."

In awe, he followed the woman to another set of double doors, where he was greeted by a gentleman who was so dignified that David felt small in his presence, even though David was taller than the man by six inches or so.

"It is my pleasure to meet you, David. My name is Ralph Power—please come in," the man said.

Inside the office, David knew he was out of place. He had never seen a desk with such remarkable workmanship. As his eyes took in the gold picture frames, he was surrounded with the rich scent of leather and realized that there had to be a misunderstanding.

"I'm sorry, Mr., uh, Power, but I don't think I belong here," he said as his eyes scanned the room. "I cannot afford ..."

The gentleman smiled. "Please sit down, David."

"Obviously, sir, there has been a mistake," David persisted.

"I assure you there has been no mistake. I can also assure you that I will not charge a fee for my services."

"I don't understand," David admitted. "You're obviously very successful. Why would you want to offer me *free* business consulting? What's the catch?"

"There is no catch," the old man chuckled. "Let me explain. Throughout my life, I have had the good fortune to enjoy success. I had lived a happy and fruitful life, creating not just a sizable trust, but also a legacy. It is just me and my wife, Linda, now; our children are all grown with successful businesses of their own. Ralph Jr. is running the legacy I have left behind. I am a natural teacher and have been looking for a worthy person to help. That's where you come in, David."

"Me?"

"Yes. You see, I have decades of experience and knowledge, all of which will die with me when my time comes. However, I know that if I don't share my wisdom with others, I would be doing a grave disservice to myself and the mentors who made me who I am. For three years now, I've been running that ad, offering free business consulting to anyone, anyone at all, and for three long years, not a single person has responded. Until now," he said, smiling at David.

"So, this is for real? You don't even know me, and you're going to give me free advice?" David clarified.

"No, David. I do not offer advice. I offer counsel. Please do not mistake the two," Mr. Power stressed.

"What is the difference, if I might ask?"

"Everyone has an opinion. Most people tend to offer it freely, although it has no merit and is not based on true experience. On the other hand, David, counsel is professional wisdom, borne solely from experience and results," Mr. Power explained.

"Okay. I get it," David replied. "I can see what's in it for me, but what's in it for you—I mean, what do you want from me?"

"I want you to take our counselling sessions seriously. In the right hands, or rather minds, the knowledge you will receive will have immense value. For that reason, young man, I am requesting your commitment to listen closely and do as I say. You must trust me implicitly, but I also must trust that you will not take our sessions or the knowledge you will receive for granted," the gentleman stated. "Now, tell me why you were the only individual to respond to my advertisement."

"Um, there isn't much to tell. I recently separated from the military after enjoying a ten-year career, most of which was overseas. As a civilian, I'm finding I don't have the skills or experience to qualify for many jobs, and when I do get a job, I somehow manage to screw it up. As a matter of fact, I was just fired a few days ago. I guess I was just at the lowest point in my life, and the ad offered a glimpse into something I can't figure out on my own," David admitted with embarrassment.

"First, I beg to differ. Anyone with a ten-year military career most certainly does have a story, and I'm willing to wager that he would also have rather impressive qualifications," the old man countered.

"Maybe you're right. My experience has proven otherwise, though. However, I will admit that I've never excelled at anything in particular," David replied.

"David, we perform at our own level of expectations. If you don't expect much of yourself, that is precisely what you will deliver," the old man said, raising an eyebrow.

"I never thought of it that way, Mr. Power," David said.

"Please call me Ralph. I think we will be spending a lot of time together."

"Okay. So what do I do? How do we get started?" David asked.

"I mentioned that I need to trust that you will value our time together and the knowledge you will gain, David. I will be investing in you and your success, but as a businessman, I need to be reasonably sure that you will be a good investment. Therefore, I am requesting that you create a video about yourself—not as you are now, but the individual you want to be and are willing to work to become. The task is not as easy as it seems. But if you accept this mission, and I hope you will, I will help you introduce yourself to the person you want to be."

3

DISCOVER YOUR VALUE

When David called Mayumi that night, he sounded like a new man. She couldn't help but smile at the excitement she heard in his voice as he recanted the details of his appointment.

"Mayumi, you should have seen his place. The guy is a millionaire—no, I take that back—he's got to be a billionaire. I'm not kidding, everything in the place had to cost a fortune. It's like walking into the Lifestyles of the Rich and Famous," he exclaimed.

"It sounds incredible, David. So, tell me what the appointment was about," she said.

"Well, remember the ad I responded to and that I was a little skeptical about it? Well, it appears this guy is legit. He said he's enjoyed a lot of success in his life and the knowledge and experience he's gained are part of his legacy. And he wants to leave that legacy with me! Can you believe it?"

"No, I can't. It sounds too good to be true. So, what is he charging you for this knowledge?" Mayumi asked, hoping David wasn't being taken advantage of, especially when he was so vulnerable.

"Nothing, absolutely nothing. The only thing he wants from me is my promise that I will listen and have a sincere desire to use what I learn. Oh, there is one more thing. He wants me to do some self-discovery and create a video, telling him about the person I want to be—not who I am now, but who I really want to be later in life," David answered.

"That sounds interesting. David, do you think you even know who you want to be?" she gently asked.

"No, I really don't. But I'm curious to find out, for my sake, and for ours, Mayumi. I do know I want to be better, and I want to do better. I don't know what my future looks like, but I do know that I cannot see a future without you in it. If you're willing to wait a little longer, that is," David said.

"David, you know I'll wait as long as it takes," Mayumi replied. "Now go do some of that self-discovery and make sure you send me a copy of the video. I want to know the person you want to be, too!"

****

After several attempts, David realized Ralph was right—it wasn't an easy task. It was downright difficult. Everything David thought of saying sounded too corny or unbelievable. He knew he could say he wanted to be a millionaire, but that was unrealistic and he didn't really think it would happen. He tried to imagine himself in different careers, but none of it seemed believable. Without a crystal ball, he had no idea what his future looked like.

Finally, he settled on something a bit less detailed. In the video, he said he didn't want to worry about money anymore and hoped he could find a career one day that he wouldn't screw up. He bared his soul, saying he was tired of being lonely and feeling like he was a loser, he was tired of not fitting in, he was tired of not having friends, he was tired of people looking at him like he is broken, and he was tired of everyone's sympathy. He said he was also tired of living with the lingering effects of war hanging over him and wished he could find the confidence and happiness that would rid himself of the demons that had taken over his life and his mind. And then he ended the video by looking into the camera and saying, "Ralph, I don't think you can help me. If you still want to try, your work is cut out for you, sir. I truly think I am a lost cause."

After watching it one time, he quickly emailed the video to Ralph as he was instructed to do, but he didn't send it to Mayumi—not just yet. Maybe one day he would let her see it, but he wasn't ready to expose all of his weaknesses to her yet. Right now, he couldn't risk losing the only beautiful thing he ever had in his life.

****

The next Monday, David retraced his trip to Ralph's penthouse, this time pausing to admire the fine details and elegance that surrounded him. It was like being in another world, a world that was so purposely and perfectly crafted that it was built to last lifetimes. It resonated with him so much that he even mentioned it to Ralph.

"It's like everything here is so perfect. Take this furniture, for instance—it's so beautiful and in such perfect condition that I can't tell if it's a gorgeous antique or brand new. It's all so timeless," David remarked.

"That is intentional, I assure you. Each piece has a place and was specifically chosen for its beauty and longevity. Beautiful things are meant to be cherished for lifetimes, David. Just like wisdom and knowledge, they should be handed down from one generation to the next, and they should be appreciated by every person who is entrusted with them," Ralph responded.

"David, this brings me to your video," Ralph said, clearing his throat.

"You were right—it wasn't easy," David interjected.

"Yes, I knew it wouldn't be. However, after watching it several times, I have to say that I don't think you are a lost cause ... but I do believe you are lost," Ralph said. "David, I asked you to tell me about your future self—how you see yourself a year, five, ten years down the road."

"And I did that," David replied.

"No, son, you didn't. You told me how you *don't* want to see yourself five or ten years down the road. You don't want to be broke. You don't want to be lonely. I think you told me that you don't want the life you're living, but, David, you didn't tell me the life you want to live," Ralph pointed out.

It made David very pleased and built trust when Ralph, a man of such high caliber, called him "son." He had never had much of a relationship with his father, and most of his memories of the time they spent together included watching his father doing drugs in front of him and reliving the physical violence he suffered at his father's hands.

"I didn't realize I did that, but I guess you're right," David admitted.

"Just like the furniture in my home here, David, you have to know what you *do* want in your life in order to manifest it. Otherwise, you'll keep getting what you've always gotten. Nothing will change. You see, it can't change when you're focusing on what you don't want, rather on what you know you really do want," said Ralph.

"I never thought of it that way," David said. "So you're saying I need to figure out everything I want in order to make it happen?"

"That's right, and you should know how you want your life to look in as much detail as possible. For example, I didn't just go out and find this desk and then hoped it would work for me. I knew exactly what kind of desk I wanted. I knew precisely how big I wanted it to be, and I knew that I wouldn't accept anything less because I was creating the perfect environment for me. You have to create the perfect future for you, as well. But only you can know what that future will look like. If you don't have any idea, how are you possibly going to make it happen? It would be a game of hit and miss, and trust me, there would be more misses than hits," informed Ralph.

"That's where I'm struggling, sir," David admitted. "You see, this is what I've always known. Besides, I'm a little afraid to let myself want something more. I guess I don't want to let myself down again and be disappointed when I can't make it happen."

"I see the problem," Ralph said, tapping his index finger on his highly polished desktop. "Let me ask you a question, David."

"Sure, what?"

"What is the value of a $100 bill?"

"Uh, it is $100, one more dollar than $99," David answered.

"No, that is not correct. What is the value of $100?" Ralph asked again.

"In U.S. currency?"

"David, what is the value of a $100 bill?"

"Oh, I know! It's 10,000 pennies!" David exclaimed.

"No. I think you've got this all wrong. Let me ask this another way. David, what is the value of a $100 bill *to you?*"

"Well, I could use $100 right now, that's for sure. It would buy me some groceries or maybe pay a couple bills," David answered.

"That's not what I was looking for, either. For now, let's suffice it to say that people view $100 differently, and they'd all do something different with it. Let's turn this around and look at the value you place on yourself, David." Ralph said. "You say you don't want to be broke, but you don't say what that means to you.

You say you want more, but you don't know how much. What are *you* worth? What's your value?"

David sat in silence, weighing the older man's response. *This is deep,* he thought, while wondering just what Ralph was looking for.

"Your next lesson, David, is to place a value on yourself—but I want you to do it twice. First, determine your value as you sit here today without any changes. Then, determine the value of the person you want to be. To make it fun, let's have a scavenger hunt of sorts, if you will. I want you to go out and find an automobile that represents you today and tell me its value. Then, I want you to find an automobile that represents you in ten years, and tell me its value. And last, find me the automobile that represents the value of who you want to be in twenty years. Can you do that?"

"I think I can!" David agreed. "If I do that, will you tell me the value of a $100 bill? You've got me wondering!"

"In good time, David. You will know the answer in good time. I promise," Ralph smiled.

4

CHANGE YOUR CIRCLE,
CHANGE YOUR LIFE

Initially, David found it difficult to complete Ralph's mission. What sounded like fun became quite a task. Drawing a blank, David lacked the creativity necessary to conjure up the type of car he was or wanted to be ... and he struggled when it came time to make an honest assessment of himself.

One of his problems stemmed from the fact that he had extremely low self-esteem. His self-image had taken a hit his entire life, and it was only just starting to heal. He knew Ralph would think he wasn't giving himself enough credit, but the old man had told him to identify a car that he really believed matched the value he had in himself right now. Internally, he believed that car would probably be a non-working vehicle thrown aside in a wrecking yard, but instinctively, he also knew that wasn't what Ralph was looking for at all.

After a couple days passed without making any progress, he decided to visit an automobile dealership, hoping that actually seeing new and used cars on the lot would spark some ideas and move things along. Pulling into the lot, he parked the car he'd purchased from his father when he returned to civilian life—an older four-door sedan that was once silver, but now was more of a faded gray. Among the shiny new vehicles that surrounded it, the car looked aged and tired. But it was dependable, and until things turned around, that would have to do.

Before he had a chance to look at any of the vehicles, a salesman approached him.

"Hi! My name is Mike," he said, handing David a business card. "Are you in the market for a car? You're in the right place."

"Um, well, no. Not really. I'm just looking right now," David answered, reluctant to tell the man what he was really doing. "I'm sorry—I really was just browsing and didn't mean to bother anyone."

"No bother at all. I'll be happy to show you around. What would you like to see?"

David was too proud to ask Mike to show him the oldest, least expensive cars on the lot, so he stepped up to a newer model, the vehicle that would represent his value in ten years.

"I'm not sure. I don't want to see the bottom of the line, and I don't want to see the top of the line. Something that's somewhere in the middle or upper-middle range. A nice, not too sporty …" David said, thinking out loud.

"Okay, let me see, you're a tall guy, so I think you might like the leg room in one of our best-selling Crossovers. It's the perfect mix between a car and an SUV. It has more room than your standard sedan, but it drives like a car. It's smooth, and the interior has some very nice touches and features," Mike said, leading him across the lot.

"Any color preference?" Mike asked.

"Something classic, timeless, not trendy," David responded.

"Black is always popular, but we have a nice gunmetal gray one, as well," Mike replied.

"My old beater over there is gray. Black would be nice for a change," David said, running his hand over the shiny black hood.

"Want to sit inside?" asked Mike.

David recognized a sales pitch, and Mike was skillfully moving him from looking at a car to wanting one. It was only fair that he told the man the truth.

"Sir, just so are aware, I'm really not going to buy a car today. I'm unemployed right now and can't afford it," he admitted.

"Oh, so you really are just window shopping. That's okay. Maybe you'll keep me in mind when you are ready to trade up," Mike said.

"I sure will. You know it is a nice car," David said, pausing to look at the sticker in the window. "It should be nice for this price!"

"You get what you pay for. This Crossover is loaded with

features. There's plenty of leg room in the front and back, heated leather seats, rear and backup cameras, a full touchscreen navigation system, cordless phone charging stations, a DVD player, and a panoramic sunroof. And, of course, it has all the accident protection features you'd want and will automatically parallel park itself," Mike advised.

"Wow. That's a lot of car—more than I need right now, that's for sure," remarked David.

"It's a great family vehicle. The wife and I bought one last year, and we love it," Mike smiled.

"That's good to know. I'm planning on getting married in the next year or two and want to start a family."

"I highly recommend it then. Are you sure you don't want to take it for a test drive? Maybe you want to see something else?"

"Thank you, but I'm sure. You can answer a question for me, though. If I were ever in the market for a top-of-the-line car, what would you show me? Something timeless, luxurious, and that has success written all over it?"

"Now, don't tell anyone I told you this, David, but if that's what you're looking for and you want the best of the best, you need to go to the Jaguar dealership down the road and check out the Ftype and Fpace," Mike confessed.

David laughed. "I like that. Mike, you've been very helpful, and I promise, when the time comes and I'm ready to buy, I'll give you a call."

****

That night, he wrote down each of the cars that represented his value over time. The first car was easy. His present value was symbolized in his current car. It was used and had quite a few miles on it. And it came with no warranty. It was one of those cars someone would buy because they needed a car, but not because they wanted that particular one. It mirrored David in value—he didn't have any particular skills or features that a company would really desire, but he was dependable.

The black SUV represented David ten years from now when he hoped to have a wife and family, a decent job, and sufficient income to invest in an upscale necessity. And while he didn't drive through the Jaguar lot, he took Mike's advice and selected a top-of-the-line, custom Jaguar Ftype that he could imagine Ralph owning.

After reviewing David's choices, Ralph was impressed.

"This is very insightful, David, and quite well thought out, I might add," he said.

"Thank you, sir. You know, I really did like the black SUV a lot. I wish I could afford it, but there's no way," David said.

"Outside of the fact that it is a family car, why did you choose that one?" Ralph asked.

"Well, I didn't think I'd be where I want to be in ten years, so I knew I couldn't go for a really high-end vehicle just yet. But it represented what I hope to be and my worth in ten years. Oh, and I chose black because it's classic and never goes out of style. Besides, the car I have now is an old faded gray sedan. If I was going to buy another car, I'd want it to be something different.

Otherwise, it would just feel like a newer version of what I already have," David said.

"That's a good point, David. You see, I wanted you to do some self-discovery and envision where and who you want to be in ten years, because that is the person you need to work on becoming. I like that you didn't merely upgrade to a newer version of what you already have. No, you chose something completely different in appearance, features, and purpose. Let me ask, David, if you were going to buy that car, what would you have to do today to make it happen?"

"I'd have to get a job and start saving money," David answered.

"Okay, and if you were to become the person who drove that specific car, what would you have to start doing today to make it happen?" Ralph asked, raising his eyebrows.

"I'd need to get a job and obviously would have to make some changes in my life," David replied.

"There you go! You must make some changes. One of those changes might be the people you associate with the most. David, besides your girlfriend, who are the people you spend time with?"

"I guess you could say I'm kind of a loner. But the people I'm most comfortable with are fellow veterans and servicemembers. We have a bond, you could say. We pretty much understand each other without having to explain anything. However, I know they all think I am weird and different," David admitted.

"Yes, the military does form tight bonds. You have to depend on each other—it literally is a matter of life or death on deployment during war time. But what you just told me brings up something else. When we first met, you mentioned that you reacted in anger to a client because yelling was acceptable in the service. Now you say you don't feel like you fit in anywhere else. David, you first have to heal your silent wounds, and you have to widen your circle. You'll never feel like you fit into civilian life if you only associate with fellow soldiers who feel they don't fit into to normal life," Ralph advised.

"But they are my friends, and I won't leave them behind," David snapped.

"And they always will be … and watch your tone with me, young man. I'm not saying you should drop them altogether, but I think you need to break away from your circle, if you will, and spend time with people who more closely resemble the person you want to be in ten years. There is POWER in PROXIMITY, and the people you associate with will have a strong influence on the person you will become," said Ralph.

"I wouldn't know where to start," David replied.

"It will not be easy, at least at first. You'll have to learn to become comfortable among strangers and people with different interests, lifestyles, and mindsets. They won't share your history or similar experiences. It might make you uneasy or even be scary for you. Push through the fear. They will help you become the person you want to be," Ralph chimed in.

"How?"

"How do they say it in the military? Adapt and overcome, David. You already know how to be a soldier, and a great one at that.

Now, you have to learn how to become a successful veteran - civilian. Break away from your circle, adapt and overcome. Meet new people who can open doors and inspire you to upgrade your life."

"Where do I find these people, Ralph?"

"They're everywhere. They are bankers, accountants, lawyers, construction workers, doctors, and teachers. They are business owners, entrepreneurs, and even automobile salespeople. Just make sure they are already where you want to be—you want to surround yourself with people who can teach you what you don't already know."

"What if they don't want to help me?"

"Successful people know there is value in sharing their knowledge and experiences. Like me, David, they get great reward from positively impacting other people's lives. Trust me, when they know you are sincere, they will want to help you. I did," Ralph said.

"I will help you get started… Let's give you another exercise to complete before our next meeting, shall we?" Ralph smiled.

"Perfect! What next?" David smiled with enthusiasm.

"There is a networking organization in town. The name of the company is Karma's Knock networking event. It's a company that helps people network with like-minded individuals. You'll meet people of all ages with different careers and interests. As a matter of fact, they are holding an event this Wednesday," Ralph said. "I will send you a text with the information. It will be a fantastic opportunity for you to break some of the barriers before you and break away from your circle, if only for one evening."

"Ralph, I'm not so sure I can. I'd feel out of place, and ..."

"David, you left your home and country and went to a foreign land for ten years. Of course, you can leave your home and go to a meeting for one night," Ralph interrupted.

"Okay," David sighed. "I'll do it—for you."

"No, David. And stop with this 'feel bad for me bullshit.' Don't do it for me. Do it for you! Do it for the person you want to be and the life you want to create with Mayumi. Do it for that! You'll never meet your future self while you're sulking at home on the couch or staying in your room in the dark, feeling sorry for yourself and waiting for someone to come save you."

"Understood, sir... Is there anything else?" David asked.

"Why, yes, as a matter of fact there is. Start looking for a job or start thinking of ways to create cash flow. Two weeks is a long enough pity party, okay. It's time to start working toward what you want," Ralph advised. "You're worth the effort, David. You need to realize this. I see something inside you that you don't even know is there. You need to work toward what you want, and the sooner you start moving, the sooner you'll be rewarded."

I have always been good at helping veterans increase their VA Disability. I wonder if they would pay me for this, or if it is even worth it? David thought with enthusiasm.

5

DEFINING MOMENTS

After the meeting, David was very nervous about going to the Karma's Knock networking event in three days. Finding it difficult to leave the house, David usually had to take anxiety meds just to calm his nerves. Leaving the house alone and going to a place with people he didn't know caused him a great deal of stress. He'd always known he was different, and his discomfort in social situations often pushed him to the side.

He called Mayumi that night. She was his comfort zone. Without fail, she understood him and accepted him, even with his faults.

"Mayumi, I spoke with Ralph again. I am learning a lot from him," David said.

"That's good, David. I think he genuinely cares. What did he say?" she asked.

"He wants me to go to a networking event this Wednesday; it's called Karma's Knock."

"Will you be going alone? Will you be okay?" asked Mayumi.

"Yes. I'm just afraid history will repeat itself. Remember, it wasn't too long ago when I went out alone to a new place and passed out from the sheer panic," David admitted nervously.

"David, your mind is strong, and you have a gift… Trust that. If you have to take your anxiety meds before you go out, do so. Remember to wear cologne. This networking is good, because you will meet people like my father. They will help you," Mayumi encouraged.

Wednesday night came, and as David had feared, he was nervous. He picked up the phone and called Ralph to tell him that he couldn't go—something bad would happen; he was sure of it.

"David, if you haven't left your house yet, you're going to be late. Let me make a call to one of my great friends. His name is Marvin, and I want you to meet him. He will meet you in the front to make sure you get in smoothly. Okay?" Ralph offered, not giving David a chance to argue.

A sense of relief swept over him as he realized he was not going to be alone.

"Thank you, Ralph. I appreciate it. I mean it. Thank you for taking the time to help me. I'm not used to that. Most people can see I'm different, and they don't take the time to get to know me. I guess it's easier to push me aside and ignore me," David admitted.

"Understood. I am in a meeting and have to go," Ralph said.

Without another word, Ralph hung up the phone and called Marvin.

"Marvin, calling in a favor… I am mentoring a kid named David Little. He responded to that ad I had up for years. Anyway, I told him to attend your event tonight, and at the last minute, he called me to cancel. I didn't let him get a word in, though, and told him you would meet him in front. I texted him your number, and he will text you when he is there. Take him under your wing tonight, will you?"

"Understood… How are you Ralph?" Marvin replied.

"Always amazing … you know me. Hey, listen, this kid is special. There is something in him. I just have a gut feeling about him. He is a ten-year Combat Veteran and worked with special forces inside Iraq and Afghanistan. He has seven deployments and has seen things we have only seen in the movies. He would rather be back at war than to go tonight. I want to help him overcome his lack of confidence and fears. He is made of excellence, just needs to find his path and why. I thought you would like him, and I know you can help him. But don't be easy on him. David needs some of that tough love you're known to hand out. He needs to find his 'why' and I think you can help just as much as I can," Ralph explained.

"Got it… Hey, I am getting another call; let's catch up over dinner and discuss a path for him. You've got me curious—I've never heard you speak of anyone quite like this," Marvin insisted.

"Sure thing, I will have Jason reach out and set something up," Ralph replied.

Ralph hung up the phone and went back to his very important meeting in his Zen garden, where he resumed his meditation.

David was sweating profusely, so much that his shirt was soaked after ten minutes. It occurred to him that being in a war was easier than stepping out of his comfort zone. But then he also remembered what Ralph had said: changing your programming is not easy. He agreed wholeheartedly.

Knowing he was going to be late, David went into the shower and sat down. He turned the shower on cool, but not cold, and focused on calming himself. He concentrated on his breathing, just as he'd been taught to do by a Buddhist monk in Japan. Feeling somewhat better, he got out of the shower and smoked a joint to calm himself more. After taking his anxiety medication and performing his breathing regulation exercises, David actually felt a little excited to go to the event.

Picking up his phone, he sent a text to Marvin… "Marvin, my apologies, I am going to be late. The traffic is horrible."

Getting dressed, David wondered what people wear to these types of events. Not owning a professional suit, he opted to wear the best clothes he had—the same sports coat and slacks he'd worn to his first meeting with Ralph. It would have to do for now, especially since he couldn't afford to buy anything new. He then got in his car and drove to the event, stopping just down the road, where he decided to leave his car and order a Lux Uber to take him the rest of the way. It would cost him $15, but it was worth it to spare himself the shame of having anyone see his car.

"Hi, Marvin, I am five minutes away," David texted.

"Great, let me know when you're at the door, and I will escort you in," Marvin replied.

"Copy. Will do, sir," David affirmed.

Promptly five minutes later, David exited the Uber.

"You must be David?" Marvin asked.

"Yes, sir. How do you know?" David replied.

"Well, you are the only one waiting at the door. Everyone else has to go through the line to buy a ticket—it's $300 to get in," Marvin explained.

David's eyes opened wide in surprise—$300 was a lot of money, and he was shocked that anyone would pay that much to attend an event that was only two hours long. In comparison, David only had $221 dollars in his bank account. He obviously couldn't afford such luxuries. Hell, he had to tell himself it was okay to spend money on food.

"Don't worry, David. I don't expect you to buy a ticket. This is my event. Tonight, you are my guest," said Marvin.

With a sense of relief and gratitude, David followed Marvin as he escorted him to a front table, next to the stage. Rather than feeling uncomfortable, David was surprised at his level of inspiration. He listened intently to the speakers, while trying to take notes so he wouldn't forget the valuable information they were sharing.

During the intermission, Marvin pulled David aside.

"What is it that you do, David? Ralph told me a little about you, but I wanted to get it straight from you."

"I have no job right now and am surviving on my military VA disability, sir," David said, hanging his head a bit so Marvin wouldn't see how ashamed he was.

"David, head up, young man. This is nothing to be ashamed of. You sacrificed your body, mind, and soul for your country. Don't ever be ashamed of that. Now, tell me, what skills do you have?" Marvin asked, taking full control of the conversation.

"Not many, sir—at least not any skills that are desirable by an employer. I know how to kill, and I'm not afraid to die. Other than that, I have no skills," David said.

"I beg to differ, young man. I've found that the military builds strong life skills—skills that would be beneficial in many different positions," said Marvin.

"Such as?"

"From my experience, I've seen that veterans do well in a number of positions. They are organized and dependable. We've hired them to fill open positions at the main office. Some work in IT, and others in sales. One of our sales guys was infantry in the Army. I have another friend that was a Marine. I will introduce you; they are both here today," Marvin insisted.

Then it was time to return to their seats for the second half of the event. To David's surprise, he enjoyed listening to the guest speakers more than he had expected. There were three speakers on the agenda, and David found them all to be interesting and confident as they told their stories. However, David silently thought their stories paled in comparison to what he had endured.

Later, he told Marvin how much he had enjoyed the event.

"You'll find that these events help you meet some very interesting people. Hearing their viewpoints and stories has been very enlightening for me. Perhaps more important, though, is that my event has been very beneficial in improving my public speaking skills," Marvin commented.

"I'm not so sure I could do it. I've never been comfortable speaking in front of large groups, outside of yelling commands," David chuckled.

"In that case, you're in the right place. Listen and you'll learn, I assure you."

In the end, David didn't make a quick exit out the back door like he'd originally intended. Instead, he mingled for a bit, making small talk as Marvin introduced him to a few of his friends, even though he couldn't deny the fact that there was still some underlying panic lying below the surface. It didn't escape his attention that he'd felt the same way in bootcamp.

What was it that Ralph had said? Ah, yes, "Adapt and overcome."

What did they teach us in bootcamp? "Push through the pain."

That was something he knew he could do, and it got him through the rest of the night.

When it was time to leave, David thanked Marvin for his kindness, and Marvin returned his words with a hug. It was a bit awkward for David, who wasn't accustomed to physical displays of affection, especially from other men. Deciding not to Uber, he proceeded to walk to his car. By the time he reached it, he was heavily perspiring once again. Blasting the air conditioning, he sat behind the wheel just as the wave of anxiety he'd held back all night hit him hard. Suddenly the anxiety took over, and David was overcome with nausea. He opened the door and vomited all over the pavement next to the vehicle.

The next afternoon, he received a phone call from Marvin, who set up dinner with him the next evening. For the first time since he'd lost his job, David actually felt a hint of hope. He had no idea why Marvin wanted to have dinner with him, but he agreed to go, although he couldn't help but hope Marvin would pick up the check, since David was scraping by as it was. David had never been to the restaurant, but he knew of it, and it was a bit pricey for him.

When he met with Ralph the next Monday, David was excited to tell him what had happened.

"Marvin asked me to dinner, and we went to a magnificent place. He liked my military background and said it really qualified me to provide security and safety at his events, and he also said he thinks I would be a great asset on his sales team. In essence, he's offering me two jobs! Then, Ralph, you won't believe what happened when I got home! I received a Facebook message from Mike, the car salesman I met last week. Anyway, he told me they have an opening for an Internet salesman, and if I'm interested, he was willing to put in a recommendation for me," David said. "But I need to give them an answer today."

"Two prospects at the same time? Tell me, David, which do you prefer?" Ralph asked.

"I have to admit I was surprised. I'm not sure what to do. I do need a job with a steady income, and I know security," David answered.

"Does the Security Officer position appeal to you?"

"It does. I have this weird feeling that I need to take this, and I think I might be good at it. It also offers some good benefits, like insurance, as well as free entrance to their events if I am not working. I will also be able to work from home on Marvin's sales team."

"Well, it does seem like you have a decision to make. You're at a crossroads right now, and the direction you choose to take will define your future. I call these 'defining moments.' Follow your intuition and trust your gut feeling. You've had them before. Deciding to join the military was a defining moment. It influenced the rest of your life. Making a commitment to Mayumi was a defining moment, and it will impact the rest of your life, as well. It's possible that going to the Karma's Knock event was also a defining moment, because of the connection you made with Marvin. He doesn't ask just anyone to dinner. He spoke very highly of you, David. I believe he sees what I see in you," Ralph said warmly.

"Wow. I never thought of it that way. So what do you advise I do?"

"I'm not going to tell you what decision to make. Only you can do that. However, I will tell you that the decision you make will determine your future. Which position will lend itself to the person you want to become in five or ten years, David?"

"Well, I don't think I want to be in either position for the rest of my working career, sir," David responded.

"And you shouldn't want to be. Defining moments aren't permanent, but they do lead you in a specific direction, and that direction will have a permanent impact on your future self. As I recall, your future self wants to be happy. Which direction will make you happier, David? When you follow that path, you'll be a step closer."

6

BE A LION—BE FEARLESS

I t was a tough decision, but in the end, David knew he couldn't handle the stress and pressure from auto sales. He didn't like dealing with people in public. Working from home seemed a better option. He was ready to try something different. Besides, he was interested in serving others, and the security officer position was a good place to start.

He thanked Mike for thinking of him, but politely declined his offer in an email. His new job with Marvin at Karma's Knock started the next Monday, and he was excited for this new chapter in his life.

A couple weeks into the job, David found that he was getting into the routine of making sales calls at home and loved attending his events for free, while being paid to provide security. However, nothing had happened that really requires his services.

Between the sales position and his commissions, along with the security position and his VA disability, David found that he was making more money that he ever had in his life. For the first time in a long time, things were looking up for him.

It showed in his voice when he talked to Mayumi, who enjoyed listening to him as he shared his days during their evening phone calls.

"Hi, baby. I just wanted to call and tell you how much I love you and appreciate you," David said with sincerity.

"I love you too, honey. Are you okay?" she asked with concern.

"I am more than okay! I am making more money than I ever have. I am starting to learn how to be a civilian again, and soon I will have enough money for us to begin our life together," he said.

"David, it sounds like you're enjoying your work. It's so good to hear a bit of happiness in your voice again," she said.

****

David had been on the job for about a month when he was put to the test. It was a night event that Marvin was throwing for displaced youth. Marvin and a few others were slated to speak at the event, which was free to the public. They didn't expect any trouble, but the event was being held in an underserved neighborhood that was rattled with violent gang activity. Any gathering in this neighborhood required the presence of law enforcement, as well as notification to city hall. They had to be prepared, and David was. When working security, he always carried his .45, which he was licensed and qualified to carry.

Marvin was on stage speaking, and David listened as he gave a very powerful motivational speech, especially his favorite part: "It is my time ... it's time to get selfish ... Become the greatest form of yourself ... You draw a line in the sand and scream 'it's my time' ..." Just as Marvin's booming voice said, "IT'S MY TIME," to motivate the crowd, gun shots rang through the air and the crowd's screams drowned out Marvin's words.

Extreme chaos immediately broke out. David's military training kicked in, and he ran as fast as he could toward the sound of the shots. Everything seemed to unfold in slow motion as he took it all in. A young man ran past him, a stream of blood running down his neck. Then David saw a woman sprawled out on the floor, obviously dead with a gunshot to her head.

Seeing the panic and level of violence, David's adrenaline kicked into full gear. He ran inside and spotted the shooter moving toward the stage. Just as the shooter pointed his gun at Marvin, who was scrambling off the stage, David instinctively lunged toward the young man, tackling him to the ground. Once he'd secured the gun, he unleashed his vengeance and began beating the shooter in the face. It was then that a police officer arrived to take custody of the suspect and subdue the volatile situation.

"What are you thinking? Why didn't you just fucking shoot him in the head?!!" the officer exclaimed.

Right then, Marvin arrived. Obviously shaken, he asked if David was okay.

"David, what were you thinking? You could have gotten yourself killed," Marvin shouted.

"I was afraid he was going to shoot you. I couldn't let that happen," David said. "I knew what I was doing, sir. In the service, it was my job to do whatever it took to save my team when shit hit the fan. It was an automatic response. I care about you, and I knew shooting him from behind was not acceptable. Plus, I wanted to hurt him. And Officer, I didn't shoot him in the head because I think death is too easy a sentence for him. I wanted him alive," David admitted.

Marvin was in disbelief as he observed how David's brain operated. With no fear, as others were running for safety, David ran straight into danger. And instead of shooting the guy, he tackled him and proceeded to take matters into his own hands, nearly beating him to death.

"Instinct took over, Marvin. I was not afraid to die. I did not want you to die, though," he responded.

"David, in the military, I'm sure you learned that you don't bring a knife to a gunfight, right? Next time, shoot the guy; he could have shot you in the face!" Marvin said.

"Well, something like that," David smiled.

Once the shooter was subdued, David and Marvin quickly tended to the wounded.

Commanding everyone to leave the premises, David pulled his gun out, keeping it at the ready. As the room cleared, his senses were heightened as he scanned the area for any additional shooters. He heard the officer say this was a rival gang shooting. David's training from combat told him that there would most likely be one more active shooter if this, indeed, was a rival gang shooting, and it was most likely that the second shooter would come from another entrance.

Quickly, his eyes swept the assembly hall for the closest entry point and the easiest one available. Identifying it, David wasted no time in moving toward the exit sign, keeping his hand on his .45. He was about ten yards away from the door when it suddenly violently opened. A man wearing a bandana and dressed in red from head to toe stormed through the door. But the first thing that registered in David's mind was the gun in his hand, raised and ready. Without wasting a fraction of a second, David yelled, "GUN!" as his finger simultaneously pulled the trigger. With a single shot to the head, David ended the young man's life.

The police officer ran up to assist David, who was standing guard at the door, looking for any other potential shooters. Seeing the body at his feet, he patted David on the shoulder and said, "Let's get this building cleared and make it Code Four."

As if they'd been working together for years, the two quickly and efficiently moved together to make sure all occupants had left the building. Once they made sure everything was secure and deemed that the building and surrounding area were safe, they called it a night—but not before the officer reminded David that he needed him to come to the station to make a statement.

"Let's call it a night. We can deal with the paperwork in the morning," he said. Then, almost as an afterthought, he reached into his pocket and handed David his business card. "Here, call me if you need anything, anytime, night or day. And thanks, man. You really pulled through for us tonight. Your quick thinking saved some lives, I'm sure."

"I guess we just got lucky that my military training kicked in," David explained.

"Luck has nothing to do with it. And you can train people how to respond in life-or-death situations, but you can't train them to be selfless and fearless. It was mad chaos in there, and you were like a lion, protecting the pride. We owe you a debt of gratitude," the officer said. "Thank you."

7

FILLING VOIDS:

FINDING FAMILY AND SUPPORT

In their next meeting, Ralph asked David to share the details of the event and the ensuing violence that took place. Ralph listened intently, never once interrupting or asking David a single question. He simply let David get his thoughts and feelings out into the open, knowing that keeping such intense experiences and feelings inside could potentially haunt David later.

Only when David had finished recanting the details did Ralph comment.

"I have to commend you for your quick thinking, David—for that and your loyalty to Marvin. I'm sure he appreciates everything you did."

"I just did what I had to do—what I've been trained to do, sir. I responded almost instinctively, but you are right about one thing: I will be loyal to Marvin. He took me under his wing and gave me a chance when I needed it the most. I'm indebted to him," David replied.

"I'm sure the feeling is mutual," Ralph returned.

"So what are we going to do today?" David asked.

"Well, I have to admit that I didn't have anything planned. This turn of events took precedence, and I figured I would just see where it took us and we would go from there," Ralph said. "Are you handling it okay, son? I'm sure it's not easy ..."

"Killing a man, you mean? No, it's not easy. Actually, it's hell. But it was necessary because that man wanted to kill others. I guess you could say I can live with the fact that I *had* to shoot him, but I wouldn't have been able to live with myself if I had allowed him to shoot innocent people, especially if Marvin were to get hurt," David admitted.

"That's a very humane attitude—one that reveals your respect for life ... and your respect for your gun. Hey, that reminds me, David, I know you're experienced with guns, but I wondered if you'd ever been hunting?" asked Ralph.

"Hunting? Oh, yes. I used to hunt, back when I was a kid. My dad used to take me. It was one of the only things we did together, and we didn't do it often. Only twice, actually. After that, I went hunting a few times with a couple buddies, but it's been a while," David answered. "Why do you ask?"

"Well, I was planning on taking a little hunting trip in a couple weeks. I have a cabin in Florida and a few acres where I can hunt pig and deer. I wondered if you'd like to come along?"

"Me?" David asked, pointing to his nose as the Japanese do. "You want me to go hunting with you? Sure! I would love to do that. It sounds like an amazing time!"

"Very good. I was hoping you'd say yes. It would do you some good to get away and clear your head," Ralph smiled.

"When and where?" David asked with excitement.

"Well, my land is in Florida. Like I said, I have a few acres there."

"How many acres?" David asked.

"1,000 acres," Marvin said.

"You have 1,000 acres of land in Florida! Wow! That's not a few acres, Ralph," David laughed.

"It'll do," Ralph smiled again as he observed David's excitement, noticing that his eyes lit up and opened wide, like a little kid on Christmas day. "Now you make sure you work it out with Marvin, and I'll take care of everything else. All you have to do is make sure your hunting license is up to date. Everything we'll need is already in the cabin."

"No problem, sir. I'm on it! And I can't tell you how happy I am that you invited me along. Truly. It means a lot to me," David said humbly.

"It's my pleasure. It'll give us some time to get to know each other better," Ralph replied. "Besides, everyone needs to get away every now and then, and there's no time like the present."

That night, Mayumi called to check on David and see how he was doing.

"Good morning, my love. How are you today?" Mayumi asked.

"I am doing great, baby. I met with Ralph again today. I still don't understand why he keeps helping me. He invited me on a hunting trip on his 1,000-acre farm. It's been awhile since I have been hunting, and I'm really looking forward to it. I always wanted to go on a trip like this with my father. He never had time for me, only beer, women, and drugs. I look at Ralph as a father figure, and I am honestly very happy he invited me."

"That is so amazing, baby! I am so happy for you. I know you always wanted that with your father, and I am sorry he was never there for you. We are your family now, and by the looks of it, Ralph is becoming a father sent from the universe to you. Remember to always respect him," Mayumi replied.

"It's funny you say that; he called me son today again. I had to hold back the tears. Calling someone son is a verbal sign that a person cares about someone. I never really knew what that was like coming from a father figure. All I could think about was what a great childhood it would have been to grow up with him as a father," David said.

"The universe is trying to tell you something, honey. Are you listening?" Mayumi asked.

"I am, my love ... I can't wait for you to come out here. As soon as I get enough money saved, I will fly you out and we can begin our lives together. For now, I have to go. I have to be up early tomorrow for work. I love you, Mayumi." David said.

****

A long winding road led them straight to what Ralph called a cabin, but to David, it looked more like a ranch. His mind had conjured up an image of a small, primitive rustic bungalow, but in reality, the "cabin" was an impressive and magnificent two-story log cabin with a porch that stretched across the entire structure. Under the porch, just above the massive entrance to this 3,500 square foot, five bedroom, three bath house, hung a huge 12-point buck.

"Well, here we are," Ralph announced. "I hope Martha has the place ready for us."

"Martha?"

"Yes, she and her husband take care of the property for me. I let her know we were coming, and I'm sure she has the place clean and the refrigerator stocked. She always does."

"I'm impressed, Ralph."

"Well, I'm not a young man anymore, but even if I were, I couldn't take care of this place by myself," Ralph admitted.

After they'd carried their bags in, Ralph gave David a tour of the cabin, showing him all five bedrooms. When they entered the game room, where he kept his hunting gear, he opened the largest gun cabinet David had ever seen. It easily held 30-plus guns inside. Ralph pulled out a specific 30.06 bolt action rifle.

"This is my rifle, David. There are many like this one, but this one is mine. You can use any of the rest that you want," Ralph offered.

After looking over Ralph's assortment of guns and rifles, David selected a modified AR-15. "I'll give this one a try."

"Nice choice. Oh, if you don't like the scope on that, I have many more. That shoots dead on the way it is. If you would like to, you can go to the range and I can have Joseph operate it for you. Joseph is Martha's husband," Ralph stated.

"Okay! I would love to get a feel for it. This was the kind of rifle I had in the military and deployed with many times," David said.

The two men grabbed a drink and sat on the front porch as David disassembled and cleaned the gun.

"It looks like you could do that with your eyes closed," Ralph noticed. "Did your father teach you how?"

"I probably can do it in my sleep," David laughed. "And no, my father didn't teach me how to care for a gun. In all honesty, he didn't really teach me much of anything, except how to do drugs, burn through seven marriages, beat women, and be angry. I did have a lot of practice in the military, though. Making sure our equipment was properly cared for was very important."

"David, I've been curious, and maybe this is a good time to ask. You rarely speak about your father, and what I've heard hasn't been very favorable. What kind of relationship did you have, if I'm not getting too personal?" Ralph asked.

David took a deep breath … Ralph could see that this was a very sensitive subject as David's eyes teared up when the subject was broached. David slowly exhaled and regained his composure before beginning.

"Well, sir, I guess you could say any relationship we did have was troubled. My father and I weren't close; we still are not. Quite the opposite, actually. Any interaction we did have usually ended up in a yelling match, and sometimes worse."

"How so?" Ralph asked.

"Let me preface this by saying my dad was a drinker, a felon, a drug addict, and a mean son of a bitch at that. And it didn't take many drinks to set him off. When he drank, everything I seemed to do was wrong. He'd start off by telling me I was stupid and yelling at me because, well, because of anything. I was supposed to know what he wanted and when he wanted it without being told. It was just impossible to please the man. Whenever I would do good at anything, he would berate me out of jealousy. And when he wasn't pleased, he was angry, which was every day. When I was young, he'd beat me senseless, and I'm not talking about the kind of beating where he put me over his knee. I can remember him hitting me with a closed fist when I was about seven. As I grew older, it got worse. I learned to leave him alone and tried to stay in my room. But he would come in, get a few inches from my face, and start yelling. He was looking for a fight and provoking me to hit him. When I refused, he would slap me, pin me to the bed, and beat me," David explained, keeping his eyes focused on the gun as he adjusted the rings.

"Didn't your mom step in?" asked Ralph?

"They divorced when I was two. He consistently had different women, seven marriages in all. There were times he would take his anger out on them, which caused them to leave. Who could blame them? I couldn't leave when I was visiting him, though. As I got older, I just couldn't sit back and let that happen anymore. There was one specific time when I stood up to him. He tackled me when I was sixteen and got on top of me, repeatedly hitting me in the face until I had two black eyes. I always tried to fight back, but that was exactly what he wanted me to do."

Ralph was silent for a few moments as he listened to David's words and observed how his body language changed when we spoke about his father. "Did you ever tell your mother?" Ralph asked.

"She knew, but she could hardly support herself, and her husband was not much better. He would abuse me, as well. When we got away from him, we were always in shelters." David said.

"Like I said, my relationship with my father was rocky at best. After a while, I grew to resent him, very much so. I'd do anything I could to avoid being around him, especially when he was drinking, which was a lot. I think he preferred it that way," David said.

"Did you two make amends when you got older?" Ralph asked.

"No. It actually got worse when I was a teenager. Once in my senior year of high school, I walked in and caught him hitting his wife—God only knows why. I couldn't take it anymore, and I walked over and beat the shit out of him. I guess he didn't realize that one day I'd be big enough to be able to hit him back. He never hit me after that day, though," David said.

"You did the right thing," Ralph commented.

"I guess so. We never brought it up again. It wasn't long after that I graduated and joined the Army. My dad is still alive, living in Butler, Pennsylvania. I haven't spoken to him in years," David said.

Those words were followed by a long, uncomfortable pause. To break the silence, David clicked the gun and said, "Here you go. I think she's as good as new."

Ralph rose from his chair and walked over to David. Instead of picking up the gun, he reached both of his arms out and embraced David, giving him a long and meaningful hug. At first, David instinctively stiffened up. He still wasn't used to receiving affection, especially from another male. But this was different. This was the type of hug David always wanted from his father. He found himself enjoying the sincerity and compassion, as well as the genuine concern behind the gesture, and allowed himself to accept it. When Ralph stepped back, he noticed that David had tears in his eyes.

"Son, not all fathers are like that. I'm so very sorry that the one person who was supposed to give you unconditional love and support failed you in so many ways. But remember, just because someone else didn't recognize your value, that doesn't mean that you don't have any. Do not let stupid minds corrupt your mind, even if they come from the one person who is supposed to love you," he said softly.

"Thank you, Ralph. I'll try to remember that. I wonder what it would have been like to have a real father, a real family, a happy family. Everything might be very different today."

"You might be right, but you'll never know. What I want you to know, though, is that you were a good son, a loyal son who looked out for the woman your father was abusing. It's a quality that I could see in you very quickly. I saw that loyalty when you agreed to my terms, remember?"

David nodded in agreement. "Sure do."

"And that loyalty was strong when you stepped up and protected Marvin and his audience at the event. You put yourself in danger because you cared about others," Ralph pointed out.

"I guess so. Ralph, do you think I'll be a good father? Or will I repeat the pattern of abuse because it's all I've ever known?"

Ralph sighed as David exposed his inner turmoil.

"David, anyone who protects others from abuse is not likely to be an abuser. That's not who you are. You are the person who protects—first your mom, then 10 years to our country and flag and your fellow soldiers, and now you're protecting Marvin and other innocent people. I'm confident that you'll be a good husband and father," Ralph replied firmly.

"How do you know?"

"Because when you speak of Mayumi, the look in your eyes reminds me of how I feel about my wife. I assure you that you won't hurt someone you love that much. Someday, in the future, I'm sure you're not going to be like your father. No, I think you'll be the man you wish your father was."

"I hope so. And thank you, Ralph; it helped to get this off my chest," said David.

"No, thank you. Thank you for sharing and trusting me with your story. I'm honored," Ralph replied. "David, I want you to know that I'm here for you, and I'll support you in any way I can. That's what friends are for. That's what family is for."

"Family? Did you just call me family?" David asked.

"Hmmm, I did. Actually, I think of you as family. As a matter of fact, I've never invited anyone outside of my family to this cabin, nor have I spent this much time with anyone who wasn't family. Now, son, teach me what you did to that gun," Ralph said.

David explained how he broke the ARA down to parade rest and reassembled the firearm. "I'm impressed," Ralph replied.

"Well, I'm pretty good at it, if I do say so myself."

"There you go!" Ralph exclaimed.

"There I go?"

"Giving yourself credit for once. I love it! It's okay to take pride in your skills and in a job well done," Ralph explained. "Now, we'd better grab a bite to eat, so we can be up at the crack of dawn and you can show me how to use that gun."

"Hey, I've been meaning to ask, Ralph, what happens if we get a deer or a pig? I mean, how are we going to get it home, and what are we going to do with it? I don't have a big freezer …"

"Oh, that's easy. I take my game to the processing center in town, and they ship me what I want. Everything else gets donated to local organizations for the hungry. They are always grateful for any support I can send their way," Ralph answered.

"So am I," David countered. "So am I."

8

LOYALTY IS POWER

For the first time in a long time, David felt like he had a place—a family, a circle where he belonged. He had felt that when he was serving in the military ... and when he was with Mayumi. But since he'd returned to the States and didn't have Mayumi by his side every day, there had been a sense of emptiness and loneliness. It felt good now to be accepted among people he admired and respected.

The only other times he felt accepted was when he was with other veterans. They understood each other, no questions asked. They all knew that each of them carried the effects of war with them, and it affected them all in different ways and to varying degrees. It was like being in a club, and only the members in it know the secrets they bear.

Once a month, a group of veterans gathered informally. It was a chance to talk and have a drink or two with buddies, and David usually enjoyed it. They'd always given him their support, and he was looking forward to telling them about his job and the hunting trip he'd gone on with Ralph.

Wednesday evening after work, David went to their usual meeting place. After joining the group at the table, they made small talk and caught up on what was going on in each other's lives. Because the guys had seen David at his worst, he was excited about letting them know things were turning around.

He brought them up to speed on how he met Ralph, and how Ralph introduced him to Marvin, who gave him a much needed job.

"It was one of the best things that could have happened to me. I really needed a boost in confidence, and Ralph and Marvin gave me that, along with a paycheck that I needed very badly," he said.

"What kind of job, David?" Blaze asked.

"Marvin is a speaker, and a really good one at that. He does a lot of events for corporations, groups, and the public. I work security for his events, and when I'm not doing that, I'm selling tickets to people who want to attend them down the road."

"You work security? Are you armed?" Blaze continued.

"Yes, I am armed. Some of these events are held in high-crime areas. When that happens, we work with the police to ensure Marvin, his staff, and the audience are safe," David explained.

Then he proceeded to tell them about the shooter at Marvin's last event. When he finished, a few of the guys commended him for his fast thinking. "Way to save lives, man!" "Marvin's lucky you were there."

But there was one vet who had another viewpoint.

"Are you crazy? After everything I've been through, there's no way anyone could pay me enough to put my life on the line like that again. This Marvin guy better be paying you a pretty dollar," he said.

"Well, he does. I mean, he does pay me—not a ton, but it's enough to get by," David answered meekly.

"Haven't you had enough of the guns and killing and nightmares, David?" the man continued. "I know I have. If you want my opinion, you need to tell Marvin what he can do with his job and find something else."

David was taken aback. It was a perspective he hadn't considered and one that he hadn't expected to be thrown at him. No, he had actually expected to receive support from his comrades, not criticism. And he didn't know how to take it.

"Hey, Marvin's been good to me. He gave me a chance when nobody else would. I owe him," David finally said.

"You don't owe him anything. If you ask me, he owes you and a lot more than he's paying you."

There was an awkward moment of silence, and the others at the table must have felt it, too, because one of them abruptly interjected and changed the subject.

"Hey, do any of you know what it takes to get disability approved? I'm getting a hell of a runaround and could use some help."

David's head turned toward the man. Not only did his question get David out of an uncomfortable conversation, but it was, in fact, something that David happened to know a little about.

"Maybe I can help you. Let's sit over there, and you can tell me what's going on," David offered, motioning to a smaller table off to the side.

***

David brought the conversation up when he met with Ralph the following week.

"It sounds like he planted a seed of doubt in your mind and you're letting it grow," Ralph remarked.

"I just hadn't thought of it like that. I hadn't even considered that Marvin might owe me for doing what I thought was right. Actually, I feel like I owe Marvin for giving me a job. Are we both wrong, or are we both right?"

"First, David, let me correct you. Marvin didn't give you a job; he gave you an opportunity. There's quite a distinction between the two, and that's where the sense of loyalty comes into play."

"Loyalty?" David asked, confused.

"Yes, loyalty. The fact of the matter is an employee can have loyalty for his or her employer, and an employer can have loyalty toward an employee. Let me explain how it works and why it's important," Ralph continued. "Some people accept a job and do what is expected of them—nothing more. To the employer, that person is dispensable. The person can leave, and they'll probably be able to find someone else to perform their duties rather easily."

"Okay," David said.

"On the other hand, there is the employee who is loyal—the one who does whatever needs to be done because they support their employer and the success of the company. They strive to do anything they can do to be a part of that success. That person, David, is indispensable. That person is what you call an 'Intrapreneur.' He or she cannot be easily replaced, and it is not because of what they do. It's because you can't put a value on loyalty. It's worth far more than a prevailing wage."

As David considered what was being said, Ralph went on.

"Now, is loyalty a one-way street? Does it, like your friend said, only benefit the employer? I'll answer that: No. You see, most employers can readily identify loyalty, and most sincerely appreciate it. It does not go unappreciated, for it is the loyal employee who gets noticed. It is the loyal employee who earns trust and is given responsibilities *and* opportunities. It is the loyal employee that people like Marvin want to keep on their payroll for the long-term," Ralph explained.

"So it's not just about money?" David asked.

"Absolutely not. As a matter of fact, the desire for the almighty dollar is often a telltale sign that loyalty does *not* exist."

"How so?"

"You watch professional sports, don't you, David? Well, there are many highly paid athletes who aren't loyal to their team. They bounce from one team to another, depending on who is willing to pay them top dollar. They do as much as they need to do to earn that money, but without loyalty, they really don't have any other stake in the game, or in this case, the team. It's each man on his own."

"But what an impact you make when you bring loyalty to the game! That's when you make a difference. It's when you increase your power, David, and that ultimately is what increases your worth," Ralph shared.

"So, you're saying it's right for me to be loyal to Marvin, instead of expecting something from him?" David inquired.

"David, only you can know what's right for you. If that seed of doubt is in your head, though, there is a way you can find the answer you're looking for," Ralph said.

"How?"

"Look to your future self. Would your future self, the person you want to be, be proud of how you interpreted your actions that day? Or would he have regrets? In hindsight, would he say that he wished you hadn't been loyal and had looked after only yourself? Better yet, if you were your future self right now, as you sit here today, what do you think you would do?"

After a long pause, David replied.

"My future self would be ashamed if I hadn't been loyal to Marvin for having faith in me and giving me 'an opportunity.' I don't think my future self would even consider anything else," David said with honesty.

"Well, there's your answer, young man. If you ever wonder if you're doing the right thing or following the right path, simply look in the mirror. If you can look your future self in the face with pride, and without regret, you'll have your answer," Ralph commented.

"David, if I can add something here, I want to point out that loyalty is one of the first qualities I recognized in you. With ten years of service in the military, you're displayed an admirable sense of loyalty for your country and fellow man. But there's more. I've heard the way you talk about Mayumi and her family, and the loyalty you have for them is profound," Ralph said.

"Thank you, sir. I could never betray Mayumi. I will be loyal to her until my dying day, and I have the deepest respect and admiration for her family," said David.

"Which brings me to another question. David, you've never told me—how did a young soldier meet and fall in love with a woman all the way across the world?" Ralph smiled.

A larger smile spread across David's face as he told his mentor about the happiest day in his life.

"I was living close to Tokyo, and on Friday nights, I usually met my friends at a pub. That Friday night, though, something was off and told me I had to leave. I just felt like something was going to happen. So I went to the train station, but for some reason, when I got to the end of the stairs in the center of the platform, I didn't get on the train right away, as usual. Instead, I walked to the end of the platform. That's where I saw Mayumi. It was like she had a white aura around her, and I was literally drawn to walk toward her.

"After we said hi, I complimented her on her necklace. I remember it well—it was a pendant that looked like a star and inside it, was a moon. She didn't know English, and I knew very little Japanese. In the few minutes I had with her, my Japanese skills were tested. When the train came, we both got on. I asked where she was going at the time, through a translator, of course. She was on the way to see her boyfriend of three years. All I could think about was getting off at the next stop and not wanting this woman to leave my life. I asked if we could be friends, and although she was on her way to see her boyfriend, we exchanged emails."

"We were friends for about nine months, talking only through email and translator. After earning her trust and respect, we went to Red Lobster in Tokyo for dinner one night. We had an amazing Chinese lobster dinner, that thankfully we shared, as I was broke and still paying alimony from my first marriage. After dinner, we went to buy fireworks. We were lighting bottle rockets, and the bottle fell down. I went running over to her, being over dramatic and acting as if I was saving her life. After that, I told her she owed me a kiss—after all, I just saved her life. She kissed me, and we fell in love that night. Three days later, she broke up with her boyfriend of four years. I know it might sound crazy, but it was like it was all part of a grand design. Whatever it was, it was the best day I'd ever had. Since then, she's been the most important thing in my life. I want to be a better man for her and for us."

"To her, I'm sure you already are, David," Ralph said. "I don't know exactly what your future looks like, but I think it's safe to say that Mayumi is one part of it that you'll never regret.

"David, can you come in here for a minute?" Marvin asked.

Upon entering his office, Marvin asked him to sit down.

"I wanted to check and see how you're doing. Do you like what you're doing here?"

"Oh, yes, sir! I really enjoy it. Providing security comes naturally to me, but I'm finding that I'm really starting to like selling more. That surprises me, considering I obviously wasn't very good at it in my previous job."

"Don't be so hard on yourself. Maybe you didn't have the right support system. I think you show promise, David. And I also think you're ready for the next level, which is why I wanted to talk to you," Marvin stated.

"What do you mean, sir?"

"I'd like to get you started in a sales training program. This training program is for high ticket sales. When you've completed it, you'll have the training and tools to be one of the top sales pros in the industry ... if you're interested, that is," Marvin explained.

"I sure am! What do I have to do?"

"Well, you have to listen and be coachable. You might be expected to put aside everything you already thought you knew about sales and life and relearn everything from the bottom up."

"Is it hard?" David asked.

"It is not difficult to learn. The key is in the implementation. To be a success, you'll have to master communication, but don't worry, the program will teach you how to do that."

"Great! When do I start?" David asked.

"A week from Monday. It's a two-week training program that's held in Denver. I'll have my assistant book your flight and make hotel reservations for you. Of course, I'll incur all of the expenses," Marvin said.

"That's very generous of you, sir. I appreciate it ... and the opportunity. Thank you."

"No, thank you, David. I learned many years ago that the best investments are those made in good employees. You're worth it."

9

BE KIND TO YOUR FUTURE SELF

Denver was the beginning of many firsts for David. It was the first time since he'd retired from the military that he'd felt like he was actually improving himself. Some of the top sales pros in the nation were there, instructing the group on how to master the art of selling, not only products and services, but selling themselves.

It was also the first time since he'd returned to the States that he was able to sit in a room with a large group of people without taking pills to combat his anxiety. Instead, David took a lesson from Ralph—whenever he felt stress or anxiety creep up, he'd take a few slow, deep breaths. Along with daily meditation, he managed to keep his anxiety at a reasonable level.

When he returned home, Marvin wasted no time in launching his sales career. He personally trained David in the company's elite ticket program and showed him how to use the professional training he'd received in Denver to boost his progress. Marvin always made time to answer David's questions and offer him a pointer here and there, and month by month, David prospered.

In the meantime, Ralph had taken David completely under his wing. While Marvin taught him sales, Ralph taught him the art of negotiation and how to increase his influence. It was a mix of business and life lessons that sometimes overwhelmed David, but always impressed him.

He wasn't the only one impressed.

"David, you're a different man than you were when I met you well over a year ago," Ralph remarked. "There's an air of confidence in the way you carry yourself. Where there was once self-doubt, I now see self-assurance. I'm impressed."

"You can see that?" David asked. "I have to admit, I do feel better about myself. I actually feel like there's hope for my future now, and I have you to thank for that."

"No, it was all you. You just needed someone to show you the way … and remind you of who you want to be and can be."

"Funny you should say that, because I was just thinking this morning that for the first time, I'm beginning to feel like I'm becoming my future self—the person I told you I someday want to be."

"I can see who that person is more and more every day, David," Ralph noticed. "And I admire him. It's been a year. How about we go back over our notes and see where you're at."

The two sat down and reviewed the person David had said he wanted to be in five years. To David's surprise, in just a year's time, he was already close to that goal. He was closing some impressive ticket sales for Marvin and had even been entrusted with training others to do the same. Not only was he earning more money, but he was making a name for himself and gaining experience that would benefit him anywhere.

Not only was he more professional and polished, but he was also a great deal more confident in sharing his views and opinions.

As his confidence and self-esteem grew, so did his income. For the first time in his life, David's bank account was at $25,000. He finally had enough money to bring Mayumi over.

****

One cold night close to Christmas that year, Mayumi called David and asked him what he'd done that day.

"Nothing new, really. Mostly, I just did the usual—closed a few sales, and after that, I guess you could say I worked on my future self," David said. "Enough about me, Mayumi, what did you do today?"

"I worked on my future self, too," Mayumi replied happily.

"Oh, and who is your future self, hon? Tell me about her," David teased.

"My future self is Mrs. David Little. Honey, I am ready to come live with you. I don't want to be away from you anymore; I want to get married," Mayumi said with excitement.

David was silent for two minutes, fighting to hold back his tears.

It was like everything was falling into place. The better he was, the more of the dream life he accomplished. After a few minutes of silence, David regained his composure.

"I would love to marry you. When do you want to come out?" David said with excitement.

"Can you buy me a ticket to come spend Christmas with you? It would be our first Christmas together," Mayumi said.

While they chatted and excitedly made plans, David jumped on his laptop and bought her a one-way ticket for Christmas Eve. He was ecstatic that he would finally be spending his life with Mayumi. For the longest time, it hadn't seemed like this day would ever come. But here it was. And it was better than he could have ever imagined it would be.

Looking back, everything he had been through was worth it because it had gotten him to this moment, this next chapter of his life. He had beat himself up and berated himself for not being able to make it happen, but Ralph had showed him the way. It was as Ralph had said from the beginning, "be kind to your future self."

David smiled, knowing that his future self would soon have the one thing that meant the most to him—his fiancé safely in his arms.

10

ADOPT A POSITIVE MENTAL ATTITUDE

D avid's excitement for Christmas was beyond what he'd felt during the holidays, even as a child. This year, he really had something to celebrate—the beginning of his lifetime with Mayumi. In a time of anticipation and happiness, however, David's anxiety kicked in, and he shared his uncertainties with Ralph.

"I'm seeing everything through Mayumi's eyes lately, and I can't help but worry that she's going to be disappointed," he sighed.

"Why would she be disappointed? She *wants* to be with you," Ralph pointed out.

"Oh, I know. It's not that. It's everything else. It's my apartment, my furniture. I'm not much of a decorator, and the place really does look run down. I just know I'm going to bring her home and she's going to be disappointed. Actually, I think she's going to hate it. What if she ends up regretting leaving everything she's ever known and starting over, Ralph?"

"David, you're always waiting for the shoe to drop, aren't you? Let me answer your question with a few questions of my own. What if she's so happy she doesn't care what your apartment looks like? What if she loves it? What if you're getting yourself all worked up about something that won't even happen?"

"But what if ..."

"David, let me stop you right there. When you were in combat, did you start every day by saying, 'Oh shit, we're all going to die today?'" Ralph asked.

"Well, no. Sure, we thought about it, but we usually went into battle hoping for the best. In everything we did, there was one ultimate goal, and that was to come out of it alive," David answered.

"Okay. Now, that was on a much grander scale when it comes to worrying. What I want you to realize is that most of the things we *waste*—yes, waste—our time worrying about don't ever happen. That's time that could be put to much better use, in my opinion."

"I get that, sir. I really do. But what if Mayumi really hates our apartment?"

"What if she does? It's not the end of the world. There are other apartments, even houses, you could make your own. If she doesn't like your furniture, maybe you could pick out something you like together. There are plenty of solutions. But doom and gloom is NOT one of them. If changes need to be made, so be it. It's not the end of the world. On the contrary, it's the beginning of a lifetime together. David, you don't have to bear the weight of everything that can possibly go wrong on your shoulders. Mayumi is going to be with you, and she's going to be your partner. You have to have a positive attitude and believe that whatever comes your way, you can work it out together."

"I guess I forget that sometimes," David admitted.

"I think you're afraid to get your hopes up, so you're always on the lookout for anything that can go wrong. And that's something we really need to talk about. David, do you know the number one reason for failure in everything?"

"What is it, Ralph?"

"It's a negative attitude. You see, when you believe that you won't succeed, you won't try. If you do try, you won't give it much effort—after all, why should you, since you already know you're going to fail," his mentor said. "It's the reason people don't try something new or take risks. They might have a great idea, but they're so certain it's not going to pan out that they never do anything with it."

"But, David, do you know what a positive mental attitude will do? Let me tell you, it's a game changer. People with a positive attitude might experience challenges, but they're optimistic that they can overcome them. When they face a problem, they pivot and find a solution. They're willing to take a risk because they believe it will bring reward, not failure. They're the people who make things happen. They're the people who succeed, and for good reason—they look for ways to succeed, not reasons to fail."

"A great way to help change your mindset to be more positive is to make yourself laugh! I learned this from my mentors, David. When you are in the shower every day, force yourself to laugh. Take 60 to 90 seconds and laugh. It really works. It changes the chemical make-up of your brain to reprogram it for positivity. Remember, David, we are all computers that are programable. It's how you program yourself that makes the difference," Ralph shared.

Ralph then turned the conversation around, telling David how to correct himself when negativity crept in, using words like "can" and "will," instead of "can't" and "won't." It was a simple exercise that, to David's surprise, really left him feeling empowered. For the first time, he actually felt like he had the world at his feet.

****

When he picked up Mayumi at the airport, he knew he had everything he ever needed. It didn't matter what happened from that moment on, as long as she was by his side.

When he brought her home, he opened the door wide and said, "Welcome home, honey, and Merry Christmas."

He'd made an attempt to make the apartment look cheerful. A dozen roses sat on a table near the sofa, and earlier that morning, he'd actually bought a Christmas tree and had decorated it, hoping to bring her some holiday cheer. Underneath it sat his gifts to her.

"Oh, David, it's perfect," she exclaimed as she hugged him tightly.

"Not yet. It'll be perfect after you open this," he said, picking up a small velvet box. Then, getting down on one knee, he said the words he'd said in his mind many times, but had never before spoken out loud.

"Mayumi, my love. This is the beginning of our life's together. I promise you I will never quit, no matter how hard times become. I promise that as long as I have you in my life, I have a reason to get up and be better. I want our future together to be amazing. I'm so happy that you are here. I know this ring is not much, but one day, I promise you, I will get you the ring you deserve, my love."

He then placed the ring on her finger, making it official. Mayumi was going to be his wife, which was the best Christmas present he'd ever received.

Marvin had given his staff the week off between Christmas and New Year's Day, and David and Mayumi spent every minute together. With her by side, he felt like he was on top of the world and could do anything, and he told her so.

"If you really could do anything, David, what would you do?" she asked.

"I'd really like to go back to school, Mayumi. I used to think that college wasn't an option. For one thing, I couldn't afford it, but I also didn't have a lot of faith in myself."

"What changed your mind?"

"You did. I want us to have a great future, baby, and to do that, I think I need to get my degree. It is just like a qualification in the military. But I also have to give Ralph some credit. He's shown me that I've been making excuses, giving myself all the reasons why I can't go back to school in order to avoid failure. I guess you could say that for the first time, the reasons why I should get my degree outweigh the reasons why I shouldn't try," he admitted.

With Mayumi's encouragement, David made an appointment with an advisor, took his placement tests, and enrolled in their local college's accelerated business degree program. To his surprise, he actually received credit for several classes and was given additional credit for the time he served in the military. Life experience was a positive in their educational philosophy. With nearly two years of credits before he even took one class, he totally forgot to be anxious and realized he should have done this long before.

"The only thing that was standing in my way was me," he told Mayumi. "But not anymore, I can do this. I can do this for me; I can do this for us."

"I always knew you could do anything you set your mind to," she said. "It's time that you knew it, too."

11

CONTROLLED ATTENTION

B etween his classes and working full-time, David had little time for anything else. Not only did he have to learn the art of self-discipline, but he also had to master it. Thankfully, he had Mayumi's full support. She encouraged him, and on those occasions when he procrastinated, she reminded him to stay focused.

However, he always made time for his regular meetings with Ralph. They still met at Ralph's penthouse apartment on occasion, but lately, their meetings were over dinner. Often, they were joined by Marvin or Mayumi, who had earned the friendship of both gentlemen.

During one of those business meetings, Mayumi told his mentors how committed David was to completing his degree.

"When he's not working, he rarely makes time for anything else," she said. "He felt really bad when another veteran reached out to him for help with his disability benefits, and he just had to say he didn't have time."

"Have you been helping a lot of guys with that, David?" Ralph asked.

"A few. I told you about one of them a while back. Since then, I've had quite a few approach me with questions. Sometimes, it's easy, but there are times I have had to walk them through the whole process and see where they're getting denied."

"It's too bad the process has to be so difficult," Marvin stated. "Isn't there a place where veterans can go to get the help they really need?"

"The VA system is overwhelmed, and it's no secret that the process is designed to be difficult. I guess that's why people turn to me. After I was denied a couple times, I got tired of it and finally sat down and figured out what they're looking for. It worked for me, and I know it's worked for some of the others."

"Like they say, identify a problem and find a solution," Ralph said.

"What?" David asked.

"It's like you've got a side business, David. You identified a problem and provide people with a solution. That's the recipe for success. Now if you could turn that into a business …" said Ralph.

"Funny you should say that because I've actually been considering starting my own business. I think it's the next logical step in my career. I would like to know how you two feel about that," David said.

David explained that he would still be able to work for Marvin if he had his own business. The business he wanted to open would serve Marvin and others like him, offering security and other services.

"In my vision, I'd like to employ veterans, utilizing their training and providing them with an income and some much-needed self-worth."

With the help of his mentors, the seed was planted and the plans began.

Ralph helped David understand the ins and outs of founding and running a business.

"Pay attention to what you learn, David, because at some point, you'll need it. The great Napoleon Hill called this controlled attention. Basically, it's using the mind and directing all of its powers toward a specific and definite end. Some vow that controlled attention is the highest form of self-discipline there is," Ralph advised.

In the meantime, Marvin was teaching him how to find and secure high-end clients, while both men were teaching him the delicate art of communication.

"It's what you say, but it's also how you say it," Marvin shared.

As David tried to soak in all of the knowledge from his instructors and his mentors, there were times when he felt like his head was spinning. It was during those times that he had to step back and use meditation and other destressing methods to clear his mind and direct his focus.

Meanwhile, Mayumi had become part of the community. She had forged friendships with the wives of veterans within their circle and had also started taking a few classes at the community college. One of her instructors approached her after class one afternoon and mentioned that she had a friend who was traveling to Japan the next year and wanted to learn the Japanese language.

"She'd be very interested in having you help her or perhaps tutor her, with pay, of course," her instructor said.

Mayumi couldn't wait to share the news.

"David!" she yelled as she flew through the front door. "Guess what? I got a job!"

"What kind of job?" David asked.

"Teaching Japanese!" she said, before she told David how it all came about.

"Mayumi, if this is what you want to do, I say go for it. But first, we have to sit down and figure out the logistics," he stated.

"What logistics?"

"For starters, you need a place to teach, and you need to know what your fee will be. You have to look at this as a business, not a hobby," David mentioned. "If you're going to do it, I think you should actually teach more than one person. You could teach a whole class and make it worth your time. I've learned a few things from Marvin, and I know a few things about getting clients ..." David said, as he turned his attention toward the woman who'd given him her full support for so many years.

****

Several months later, David found himself alone one evening while Mayumi was teaching. He didn't feel like microwaving anything for supper, so he picked up the phone.

"Hi, Ralph! Hey, Mayumi is teaching tonight, and I was wondering if you wanted to go somewhere and grab a bite to eat. I feel like it's been weeks since we last talked, so this would give us a chance to catch up," he said.

"Normally, I'd love to, David. But I just can't tonight."

Suddenly, David noticed that Ralph's voiced sounded weary.

"Everything all right, Ralph?" he asked with concern.

"Oh, I'm sure I'll be fine. I've just been a bit tired recently—I'm not getting any younger, you know," he answered.

"I'm serious, Ralph. Have you seen a doctor? Can I do something for you? I can bring you something to eat if you want. Maybe—"

"That's not necessary, David," Ralph interrupted. "I haven't had much of an appetite, anyway. And don't worry about me—I've made an appointment with my doctor. Like I said, I'm sure everything's fine."

"I sure hope so. I'll check in with you tomorrow and, Ralph, if you need anything, don't hesitate …"

"I won't, David."

****

A few days later, Ralph texted David.

Just wanted to let you know I'm in the hospital. Nothing to worry about. Just running some tests to rule a few things out.

David couldn't help but worry. In fact, he was beside himself with worry, and when he told Marvin, his boss couldn't hide the obvious concern that passed over his face.

"We'll just have to pray—and wait and see. I can tell you Ralph's a tough one. There's nothing that's going to keep him down for long," Marvin said.

When Ralph was released from the hospital, he asked David to stop by—and that's when David could tell something really was wrong. Right away, David noticed that Ralph looked pale and had lost weight.

"David, I told you when we first met that I would be honest with you, and I meant that. I know you've been concerned about me, and I feel it's only right that I let you know what's going on," Ralph said.

"What is it, Ralph?" David asked softly.

"I've been diagnosed with cancer, David. But I don't want you to worry. I'm a fighter, and I'm going to do everything the doctors tell me," Ralph advised.

"Ralph, I will be here for you, no matter what you need. You won't go through this alone—we will fight this together," David promised as he fought back tears.

"I know that, son, and I appreciate it. It might not be easy, but nothing worthwhile ever is. I'll still be here for you, as well.

You've grown to mean a great deal to me. But there will be times when I might have to be selfish and focus on my health. I know you understand."

"Of course I do. And that's where your attention should lie from this moment forward. It probably won't be easy, since you're such a selfless man, but I want you to be very self-disciplined when it comes to your health. Lean on me and let me help you. Starting this very minute, focus your attention on your desired end result, and I will, too," David vowed.

"Thank you, David," Ralph said as he reached across and touched his mentee and friend's hand "And can I point something out?"

"Sure," David replied.

"As we're sitting here today, it's occurred to me, David, that you're starting to sound like me," Ralph said with a soft chuckle. "I hope you view that as a good thing."

"It's not a good thing, sir," David commented. "It's a great thing and the best compliment you could have ever given me. Ralph, you're more than a mentor—you're like the father I never had. You've done so much for me. Now it's my turn to be there for you."

"I'm glad you said that. I've taken the liberty of making a copy of my chemotherapy schedule for you. Depending on how chemo affects me, I may need to count on you for a ride to my treatments from time to time," Ralph said, handing David a copy of his calendar.

"Don't you worry about a thing. I'll take care of anything you need. Just keep a positive mental attitude and put all your energy toward getting well," David reassured.

"Just like me," Ralph mused. "I swear you sound just like me."

12

DEFINITION OF

LIFE PURPOSE AND SUPPORT

I t's been said that it's the moments when we are tested that we become stronger, but David quickly learned that there was more to it—it's the times when we are tested to the max that we find our purpose and *that's* what makes us stronger.

A few months had passed, and David had opened his own business on a part-time basis while he was completing classes toward his degree. This offered him the flexibility to accompany Ralph on nearly all of his chemotherapy treatments.

Ralph usually took these opportunities to share stories about his businesses, his family, and his life. David learned about Ralph's parents and his childhood. He listened as Ralph spoke with pride about his children and grandchildren.

Ralph was scheduled to have chemo for 26 weeks. Somewhere around the sixth week, he blurted out something unexpected.

"I have no regrets, David. I want you to know that."

"That's good. I wish I could say the same," David responded.

"No, I meant I don't regret my desire to offer to mentor you. On the contrary, it's one of the best things I think I've ever done. Like I told you initially, my reasoning at the time was to create a legacy by sharing my knowledge and experience. But it's become more than that, don't you think? I think along the way, I benefited from it as much as you have," Ralph shared. "I'm truly glad to have you in my life, not just as my mentee, but as my friend. Watching you grow, I really feel that you're destined for greatness. Promise me you'll stay focused."

Listening to Ralph's words, David choked up, so much so that he couldn't trust himself to respond to his kind words. Instead, he simply nodded his head, letting Ralph know that he heard every word and wouldn't forget them.

That night, he told Mayumi about the conversation.

"Babe, I just wish I knew what to say. Instead, I didn't say anything. Sure, I was trying to fight back tears, and I think Ralph knew that, but I should have told him how I really feel. But I didn't."

"You still can, David. There's nothing stopping you from telling him how you feel now," Mayumi softly reminded him. "If it's uncomfortable or you don't trust yourself to be able to get the words out, why don't you try writing him a letter?"

That night, David poured all of his feelings out onto a piece of paper. One might think that it encompassed pages and pages, but in reality, it was short on words but very large in sentiment.

The opportunity to give it to Ralph came at the end of chemo the next week. David's hand shook slightly as he handed the letter to the man he grown to love and respect.

"Here, I was very touched by the things you said last week and wanted you to know how I feel, as well."

Ralph reached over to the table next to his recliner for his reading glasses. After breaking the seal on the envelope, he read David's carefully worded letter.

Dear Ralph,

Forgive me for not expressing my true feelings last week. I was touched and overcome with emotion at the time. I want you to know that your influence and impact on my life has been tremendous, and in more ways than one. I can honestly say that I look upon you as a father—not the one I had, but the one I've always wanted. I know I am not your son, but I just wanted to let you know that I love you like a father and would do anything in my power to help you or anyone in your family.

Love,

David

This time, it was Ralph who wiped a tear from the corner of his eye. This time, it was Ralph who was at a loss for words and could only nod in response.

When David pulled up at Ralph's door, Ralph asked him to come up to his penthouse for a minute.

When they got on the elevator, Ralph cleared this throat and said, "David, I look at you as a son and love you as one, as well. I hope you know this. I know your father reached out to you yesterday for the first time in years, and it resulted in a terrible blowout. I want this to be the last time you have to go through that. It's time to change your stars, son. You have my permission to change your last name to Power. I would be honored to call such a great person my son."

As he realized what had just happened, tears openly fell down David's cheeks. Again at a loss for words, he simply mumbled "yes," before giving Ralph a hug, which was reciprocated in a way that David could only imagine a loving father embracing his son after returning from deployment.

"It's my pleasure. There is something else, though, that I want to give you. I was going to wait, but it seems like it's the perfect time," Ralph said, as he unlocked the door.

David followed Ralph as he walked into his office. After unlocking his desk drawer, he reached in and pulled out an envelope.

"David, I also wrote you a letter, but do me a favor and don't open it until you get home," Ralph said.

"What is this?" David asked, confused.

"It's a letter, that's all you need to know for now. Well, that and one more thing," Ralph stated.

"What's that?" David asked.

"Let's just say great minds think alike," Ralph smiled. "Now go home, son. Go home to Mayumi."

David insisted that Mayumi stay by his side while he opened the letter. Uncertain what Ralph had to say, he was also unsure how he would respond to it. After opening the envelope, he also knew there was no way he could have prepared for what was in it. A check for $50,000 fell onto his lap, and this time, it was David's hands that shook while he read the letter.

"To my son,

Change your stars, start your business and life with Mayumi.

I love you,

Dad"

13

CREATIVE VISION

From that day forward, the trajectory of David's relationship with Ralph changed. No longer were they two men who simply admired and respected each other, though they most certainly did, but they now had a bond—one that was unbreakable, the bond of a father and son.

It wasn't always easy, but Ralph completed his chemotherapy treatments, which were followed by weeks of radiation, and through it all, David was by Ralph's side for the treatments, as well as anything else he needed. It was the least he could do for the man who had done so much for him.

Above all, David knew the one gift he could give him was to become a success. The generous $50,000 Ralph had given him allowed David to launch his business on a full-time basis. With the assistance of Ralph and Marvin, he created a high-profile security company, and he knew he couldn't have done it without them.

It was Ralph who connected him the people who could provide him with referrals. With glowing recommendations from Marvin and Ralph's endorsement, David soon began accumulating a stream of high-profile clients, including well known celebrities, government officials, and wealthy business people and their families. Because of David's long and respected military career, they trusted him and the veterans he hired to maintain confidentiality, while being professional and dedicated to keeping them safe.

Just as things were taking off for David, though, Ralph got bad news. His latest CT scan showed that not only had his cancer returned, but it had spread to other areas of his body. Ralph took the news admirably, but he knew it was not good and without mincing words, he came right out and asked his doctors about his prognosis.

"How much time do I have?"

"With treatment, about a year and a half," the doctor replied somberly.

It was a lot to take in, but Ralph had never been one to give up, especially when times got tough. After he took some time to accept his outcome, he set his mind to living life on his terms. If he only had 18 months, he wanted to make the most of it in every way he could.

He dove in and taught David everything he knew at every opportunity. However, he didn't share his prognosis with him ...

not yet. First, he wanted David to focus on making his own vision, his own dream, come true.

As David's success unfolded throughout his first year, Ralph couldn't help but feel an immense amount of pride for the role he had played in helping this man who he now looked upon as a son. But even more, he had so much pride for David and the tremendous strides he had made since the day they first met.

Ralph had watched David grow throughout the years, and during this first year as a business owner, he had watched David's business grow, as well. It was one of the most remarkable successes Ralph had the pleasure of contributing to. But he had to give much of the credit to David for having the vision and being able to turn it into a swift success. At the year's end, they were both astounded that the original $50,000 investment had grown to $2.5 million dollars.

That hadn't been easy, either. David had poured himself into the company, working 20 or more hours a day at times. But it had paid off in a big way. In his first year, David had made a clean $500,000 profit after he had paid all of his employees, and that was quite an impressive accomplishment.

David did offer to reimburse Ralph for the $50,000 investment, but Ralph flat out refused. Watching David's life come together was all the reward Ralph really needed and he told him so as often as he could.

The two would talk on the phone frequently and made it a point to get together a couple times a week. They talked about work, family, and the future, but mostly they enjoyed spending time together, as a father and son would. They celebrated his milestones together, especially when David legally changed his name, and then when he made the announcement that Mayumi was expecting their first child—a baby girl.

"Did you know all of our granddaughters have my wife's name as their middle name? Every one of them has the middle name 'Lynn,'" he stated.

David nodded, indicating he understood what Ralph was telling him.

****

That day came when David received an unexpected phone call from his biological father. A national magazine had mentioned David's company and his success in an article, and apparently, someone shared it with his father.

When David answered the phone, he recognized the voice immediately.

His father didn't waste any time, but got right to the point. He needed money. After all, he was his father, and David owed him that.

David was very careful to keep his voice calm.

"You've never been a father, and I don't owe you anything," he remarked.

Suddenly, the tides turned and his father unleashed all of the pent up hatred he had in his heart on his son.

"You've always been a disappointment to me. I can't believe I could actually have a son who is such an ungrateful fucker. I was right to push you out of my life years ago. You're worthless, David, and I'm ashamed of you. If I was there right now, I'd beat the shit out of you. I should have done it when you were a baby. You know what, I don't want anything from you. The best thing you can do for me is to stay out of my fucking life. Drop dead!"

David held the phone away from his ear as his father screamed at him. When he finished and David could get a word in, David started to shout back, but then had second thoughts. Why? What was the point? Would it do any good? And above all, was there anything he could say that would even matter—to David or his father? Knowing the answers to all those questions, David took a deep breath and experienced his greatest test in patience as he gently hung the phone up.

His father's vicious words repeated in his head as he contemplated how anyone could harbor so much hatred for their own child. Then he realized it didn't matter. His father didn't matter. He had Ralph, and Ralph was the family he'd always imagined, the one he'd always wanted.

He picked up the phone again—this time, to talk to the man who had the greatest influence over him. Ralph listened as David shared the conversation that had just taken place, and for the first time, David thought he detected a stern note in Ralph's voice.

"That's enough of this shit. That bastard is your creator only, and he doesn't even deserve that. Block his damn number."

The next day, he and Mayumi met Ralph and his wife, Linda, for dinner. That's when they shared Ralph's prognosis with them. It was also when Ralph made a very specific request of David and Mayumi, one that would make the daughter they were expecting a part of the Power family.

"Should you give me any granddaughters, I ask that their middle name be Lynn, after my lovely wife, Linda. In that way, David, both you and your future daughters can be part of our legacy."

14

HEALTH AND WELLNESS

It was the middle of the week, and as he often did, David popped in to pay Ralph a visit.

David's life had changed immensely since he'd started his security company. Gone was the young man who had walked through those very doors wearing the only sports coat he'd ever owned. The man who stood before him was the picture of success. Wearing an impeccably tailored $2,000 Armani suit, David's left hand now sported an impressive custom made wedding band. And the car that he'd once been so ashamed of had been replaced by a gleaming new Jaguar F-Type, also custom made.

David was more than a success; he was a wealthy man who had established himself in the business community. He had accomplished so much more than his five-year vision, for now he was not only a successful business owner and husband, but he had gained a new title: Daddy. Mayumi had given birth to their first child, a girl, and living up to his promise to Ralph, they had named her Maya Lynn Power.

Ralph beamed with pride as David shared pictures of his daughter, who he obviously adored.

"She is absolutely beautiful. Take care of her always," Ralph said.

"Oh, I will. She won't want for anything; I promise you that."

"I'm certain of it, but don't forget, son, there are some things money cannot buy, and I'm a perfect example of that. I have enough money to last several lifetimes, maybe more, but I can't buy back my youth. I cannot buy back my health and vitality."

"I wish I could give those back to you," David commented.

"Oh, I know you do. But in all truthfulness, I have no regrets. Sure, I'd like to be graced with a few more years, but I have been very blessed with what I've been given. David, yesterday, the doctor told me that I'm nearing the end. At best, he believes I only have a few more months," Ralph informed him.

"That's all? There's nothing else they can do?"

"They've done everything they can, son. That's all we can ask of anyone. I've lived a rich and full life, and now it's time for me to pass that torch on to you. But when you're in your twilight years, like me, I don't want you to have any regrets, either. Enjoy all the things success can buy, David. Become a man of influence and make a difference whenever and wherever you can. Take care of Mayumi and your beautiful baby. But along the way, don't forget to take care of yourself. Your body is the one thing you have that can't be replaced. In the end, it is the one thing that you cannot live without. Give it the respect and attention it deserves."

"I will," David promised.

"In my younger days, I was much like you, David. I worked incredibly long hours and thought sleeping was a waste of time. I grabbed lunch on the go, if I even took time to eat. Everything was at such a fast pace that I neglected to take care of the one thing that was necessary for anything else to happen—me. I should have exercised more, eaten healthier, and made time to relax and enjoy the fruits of my labor. Don't get me wrong, I eventually did all those things, but I didn't recognize the value of my health until it was too late," Ralph remarked.

"Don't be so hard on yourself," David replied.

"I'm not. The point is, I was too hard on myself in my younger days. I took my health for granted, thinking it would never fail me. I was wrong. The one thing I neglected is the one thing I now value most," Ralph said.

"Perceived value can change. I remember you telling me that ... what were you talking about back then? Wait! I remember—you asked me to tell you the value of a $100 bill. And I gave you every answer I could possibly think of, but none of them were right. You never did tell me, what is the value of a $100 bill?" David asked.

"Like your health, it is whatever value you give it at the time. David, when you first came to me, I bet $100 meant a lot to you, didn't it?"

"It sure did! I barely had two nickels to rub together."

"Well, tell me, what is the value of a $100 bill to you now?"

"The value of $100 is, well, $2,000 can buy you an Armani suit ..." David still could not find an answer he wanted.

"One day you will figure it out, David." Ralph said

"Stay true with your health, even your life, son. What you take for granted one day might be the most important thing to you tomorrow. Don't let it be your health and wellness, son, because those are two things money cannot buy. When they're gone, you can't always bring them back."

As Ralph spoke, David was pained to listen to the finality in Ralph's words—he was leaving him with life lessons as he entered the last stage of his own life.

"David, while I can, I'd like to make one last trip to the ranch. Do you think you and Mayumi can manage to get away and join me next week? With the baby, of course," Ralph asked.

"There is nothing we'd rather do," David answered.

****

David was distraught when he got home as he took in everything Ralph had said. It had been a somber conversation and one he knew was important to Ralph, but it only served to cement the reality that David was losing the man who meant more to him than any other in his lifetime.

It occurred to David that Ralph was right—money cannot buy good health or wellness. But David realized there was one more thing it couldn't buy—time.

15

CREATE A LEGACY THROUH ADVERSITY, DEFEAT, AND TEAMWORK

The week spent at the ranch gave them all some much needed time together. Ralph and Linda both doted on their granddaughter, and the memories were captured in plenty of pictures. It was time well spent, and David knew he'd cherish it forever.

Once back home, Ralph rarely left his house, spending most of his time with Linda. It was all he had energy for anymore. A trip to the doctor would leave him exhausted for the rest of the day. David and Mayumi were visiting him daily, making sure he was comfortable and didn't need anything, but mostly enjoying the time they had left.

One Sunday afternoon, David walked in and noticed that Ralph didn't look well. He looked frail and his face had an evident pallor to it. David's heart dropped as he looked Ralph in the eye, and Ralph knew that David could tell his time was nearing the end.

"Sit down, boy. Let's talk," Ralph said.

"Sure, Pops. What's on your mind?" David asked with concern.

"I'm proud of you, David. I hope you know that."

"I do," he assured him.

"Promise me that you won't ever quit. Not under any circumstances whatsoever. If there is one thing I can attribute my long-term success to it is the fact that I didn't give up. Like the lions outside my door, I've been a fighter. Stay true to Mayumi, as I have been to Linda. She will be there for you, like Linda has been for me. They both are amazing women for putting up with our asses. Don't you ever quit on her. There will be tough times. But do not ever quit on her or your baby girl, Maya," Ralph said with all the earnest he could muster.

"I won't quit, Pops. I promise," David assured him.

Ralph explained that there would always be times when the going gets rough. With the good always comes the bad. You need one to appreciate the other.

"Life is like a roller coaster, son. Sometimes you're scared to death, and sometimes you're on top of the world feeling a rush of excitement. But if you can face adversity without fear, you can get through it," Ralph explained.

"But you can't get through it alone," Ralph continued, pausing to catch his breath. "You need a team, people on your side—like you have been to me."

David listened as Ralph's words grew slower and slower. As he drifted into sleep, he patted David's hands and muttered what would be his last words to David, "That's my legacy to you, David. Above all, be kind to yourself. If you do that, you'll be a winner. I love you, son."

Tears ran down David's face as he held Ralph's hand until he drifted off to sleep. When Linda walked into the room, he whispered that Ralph was sleeping, and David and Mayumi each gave her a warm hug as they were leaving.

David mentioned to her, "He still won't tell me the value of $100."

"Silly boy, the value of $100 is whatever you make it to be. Just like your life, make it what you want. Drive safe and text me when you get home," Linda stated, giving David the one answer that Ralph hadn't had time to.

****

The next morning David received a call from Linda. She said she woke Ralph us the night before, telling him good night and letting him know she loved him. He was coherent and without pain, saying only, "I love you, Linda.= Thank you for dedicating your life to me." He then went back to sleep and passed away that night. After hearing the news, David told her how sorry he was for her loss and let her know that if she needed anything, they were just a phone call away.

Then he turned to his wife and as they cried, he sought the comfort he very much needed in her embrace.

As he began the process of mourning, David relived the years they'd spent together and the memories they'd made. Just as Ralph had been by his side through his most trying times, David was thankful he could say that he had been loyal to the man who had become not only his mentor, but his father, until the very end.

16

PASSING THE TORCH

It was a year and a half after Ralph's death, and after having a horrible fight with Mayumi, David took some time alone to go through Ralph's meeting notes. He reviewed everything that he had written down, and as he did, he remembered himself back then. Recalling how negative and anxious he once was, he knew the vast impact Ralph had on his life.

David knew he wanted to do something to carry on Ralph's legacy, but to him, his father's legacy was so large that it was impossible to pinpoint any one thing to memorialize the man.

As he sat with Mayumi, making amends, David looked around at their beautiful house and the two daughters they now had: Maya Lynn Power and Mia Lynn Power. He recalled how impressed he'd been the first time he had walked through the doors to Ralph's office, remembering that day for what it was—a pivotal moment in his life. The lions that had so stately adorned the side of each door had made such an impression on him that he had purchased two similar, equally grand lions for their own house. His glimpse into the past also revealed some of his most difficult times, but with the bad also came the good, and he caught a glimpse of the love in his eyes when he looked at Mayumi.

Because of the kindness of one man, David was an entirely different person than he'd been four years prior. In David's mind, there wasn't anything he could do in Ralph's memory that could come close to what Ralph had done for him.

Then, it hit him. He could carry on in his chosen father's footsteps. Ralph was gone, but David realized that his wisdom and lessons didn't have to die. And he wasn't going to let them.

Opening his phone, he created a new social media page, put a general picture on it, and titled it simply, "Business Consulting."

Then he created one ad, with no posts, no page history, no information, just as Ralph had done, and set it on auto pilot for the next five years.

Free Business Consulting – No Strings Attached – Call This Number

Now, he had nothing to do but wait and live his ultimate dream life with the family he always wanted. He didn't know when, but he knew that one day, when the time was right, the universe would provide a worthy student to carry on the POWER legacy.

ABOUT ERIC POWER

E ric Louis Power served honorably in the United States Navy from 2002 to 2012. During his years of service, Eric reached the rank of Petty Officer First Class. He has served in Operation Iraqi Freedom, Operation Enduring Freedom, and Operation Southern Watch. Eric has a total of seven deployments, with 3.5 years in Active Combat zones.

A merchant at heart, Eric created Veterans Disability Help, LLC while pursuing his first business degree. He is a co-author of the bestselling book, Power of Proximity. Don't Shoot Your Future Self is the first book he has solely authored and published.

Eric has a passion for helping everyone, including his brothers and sisters in arms. He is a standing Board Chairman for the nonprofit "Brighter Future Charity," where the focus is helping children on the spectrum gain valuable social life skills. (http://www.brighterfuturecharity.org/)

Eric is a husband, father, and disabled veteran. When he is not working as the Chief Executive Officer in his firm, Veterans Disability Help, LLC (https://veterandisabilityhelp.com/lions-den/), he is either with his family or can be found in the woods hunting whatever is in season and recalling the lessons taught to him by his first mentor, Ralph Power.